For Clarissa

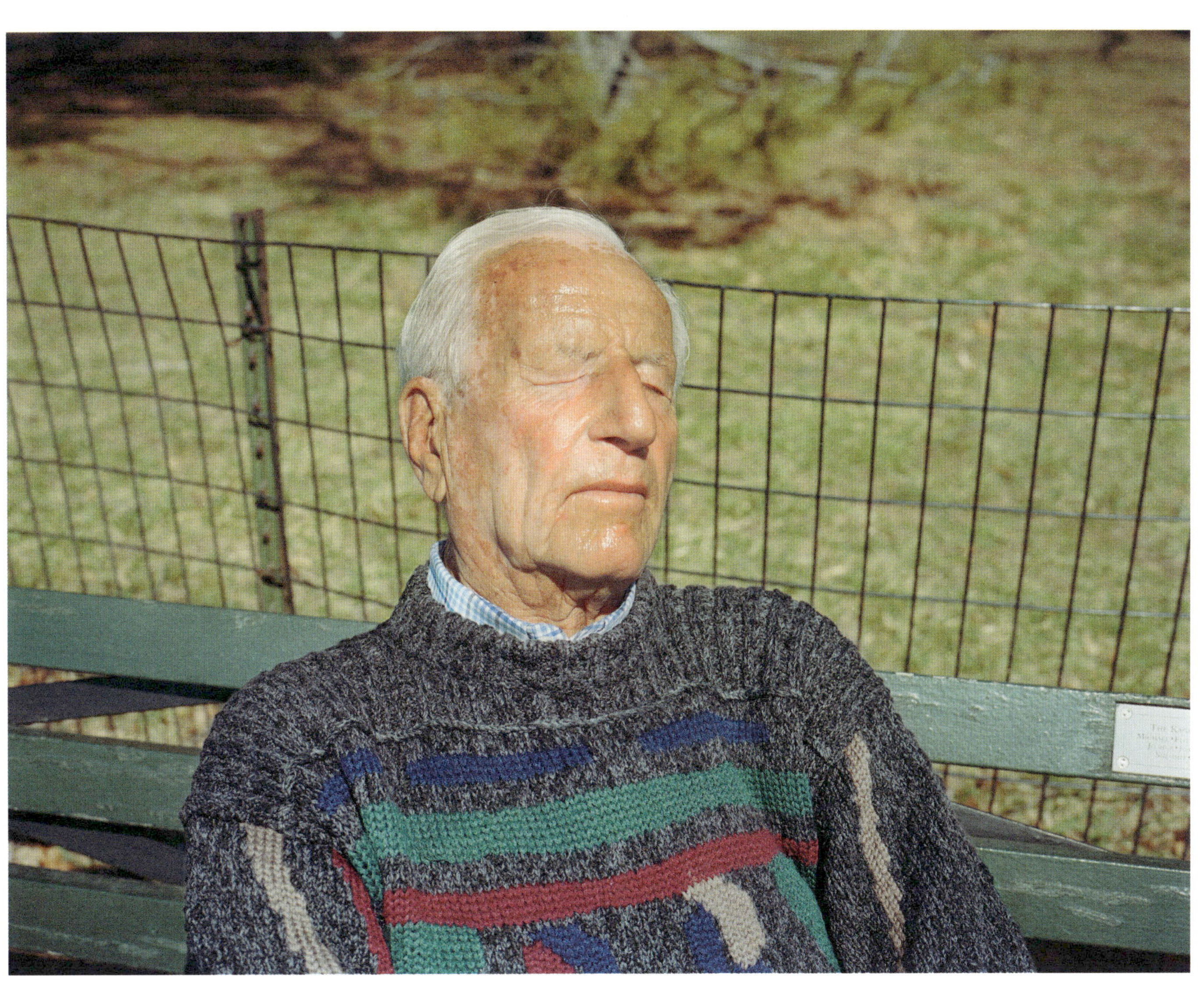

Scott Rossi

COMMON PLACE

Pomegranate Press

Guest Editions

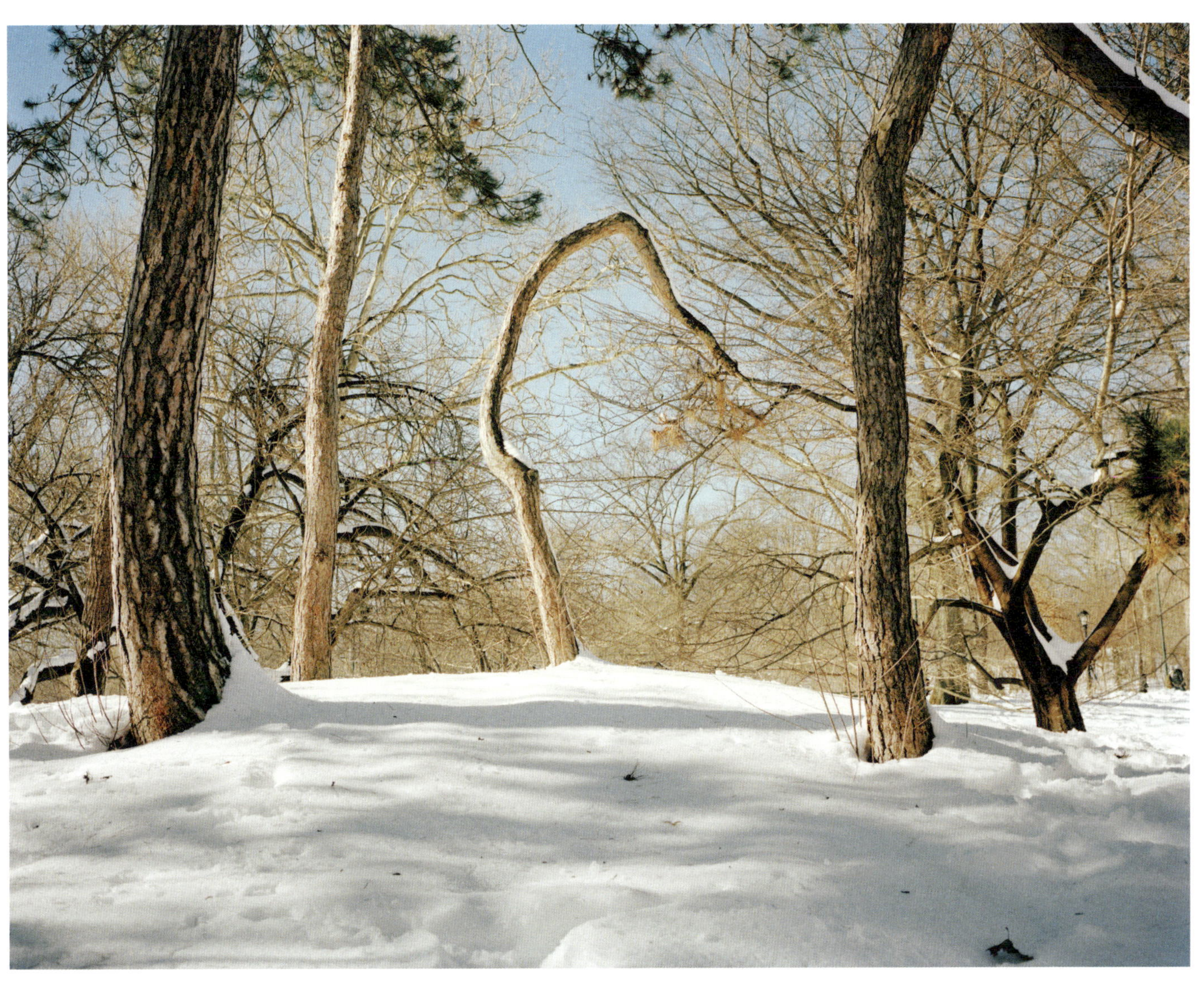

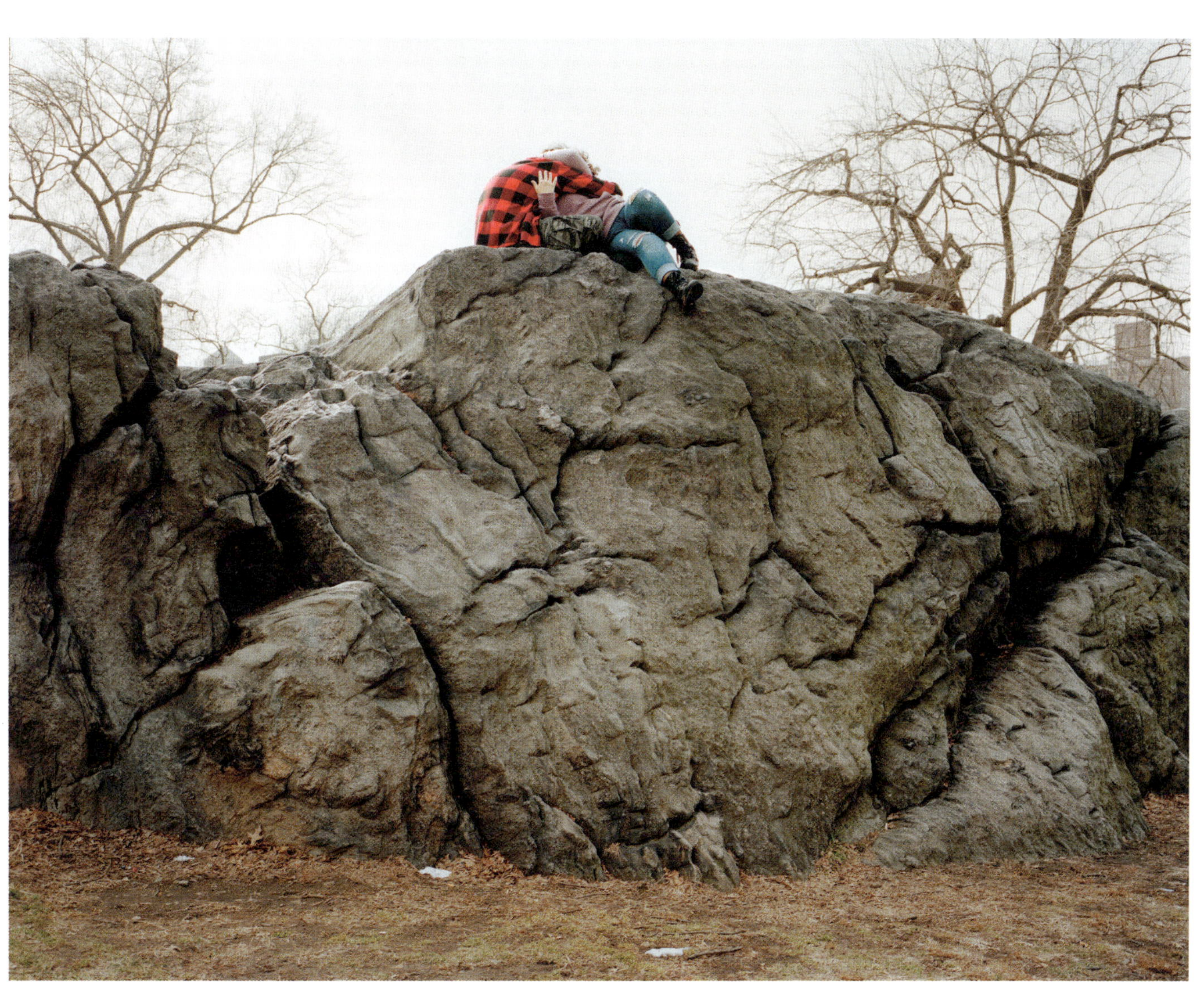

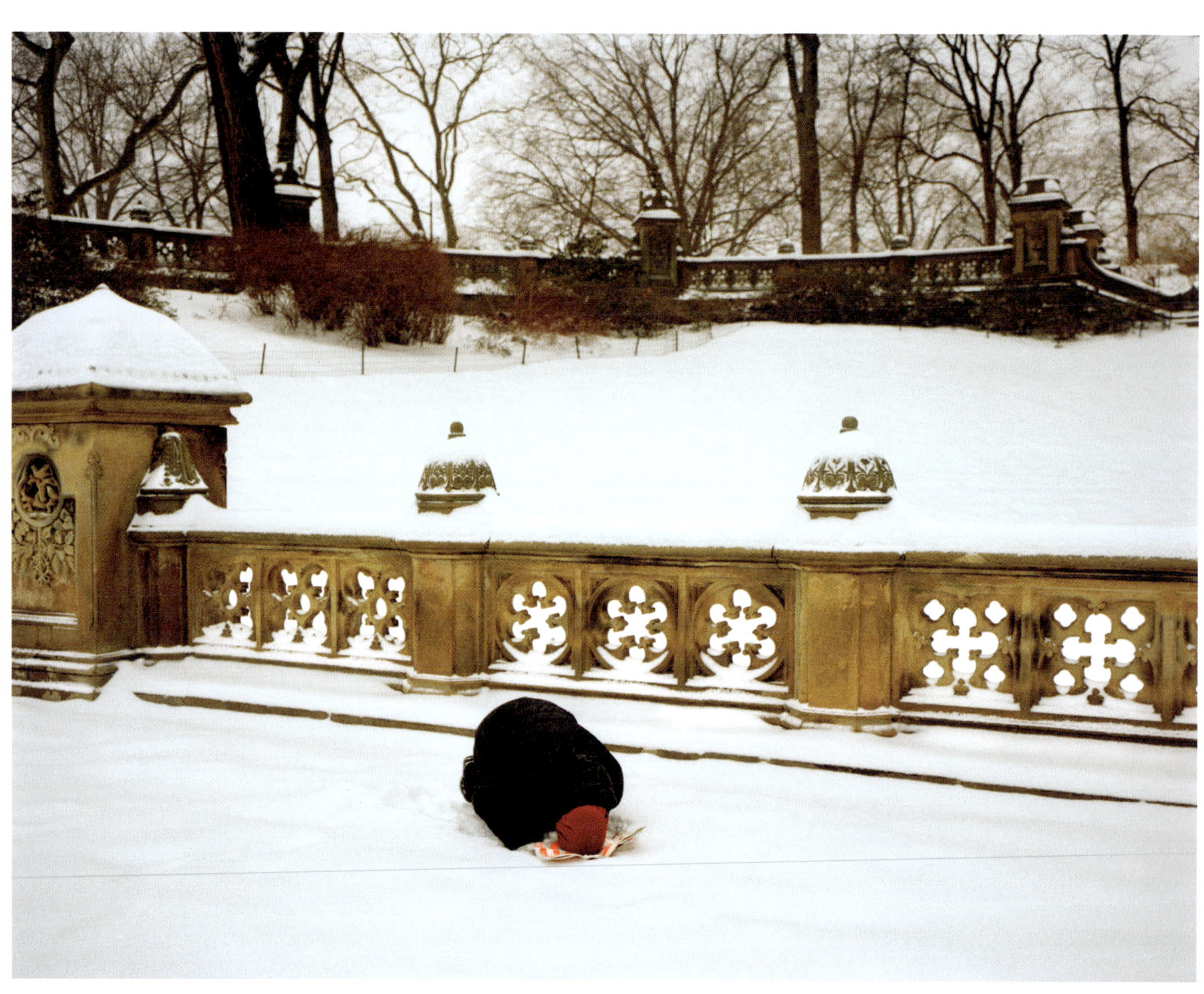

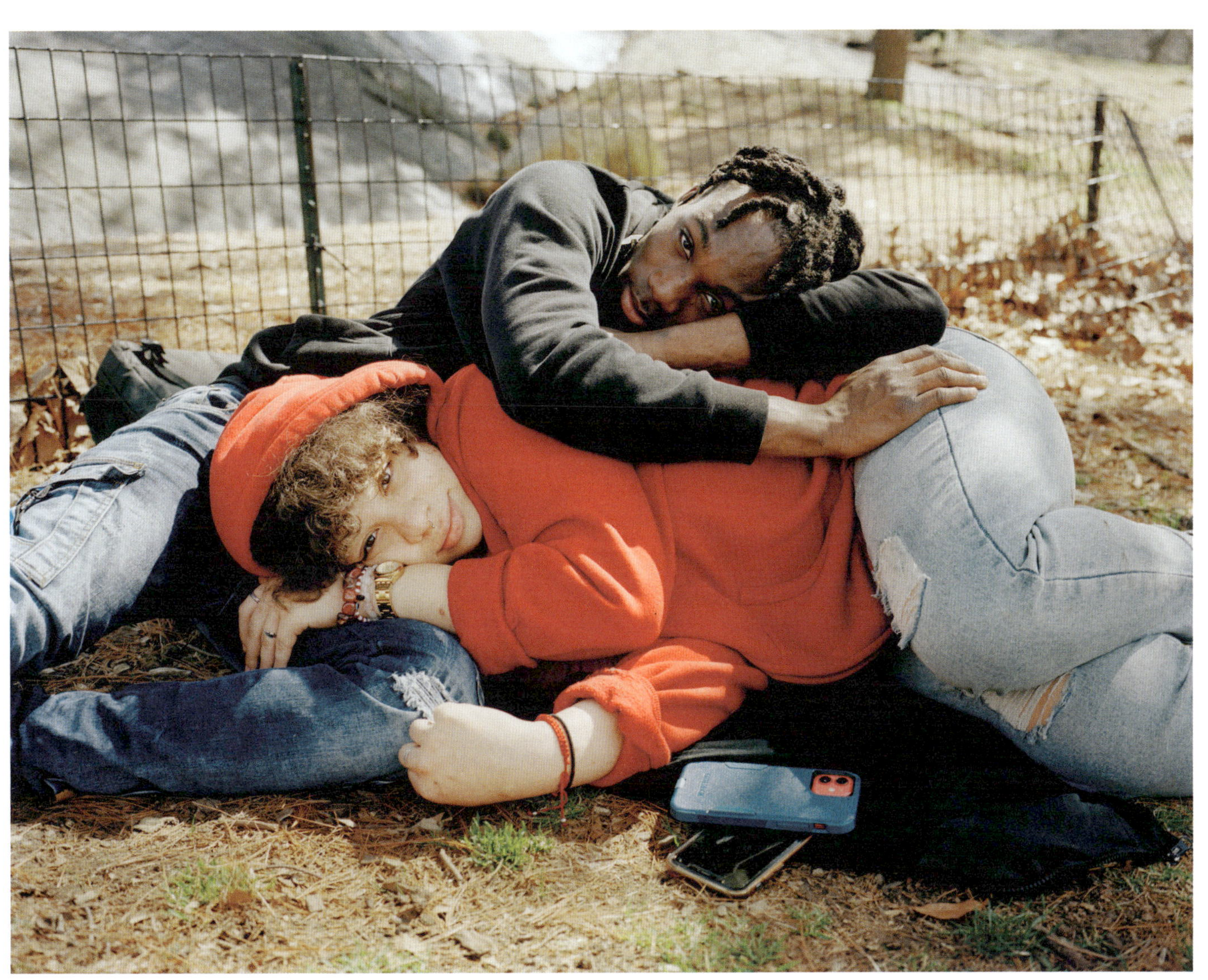

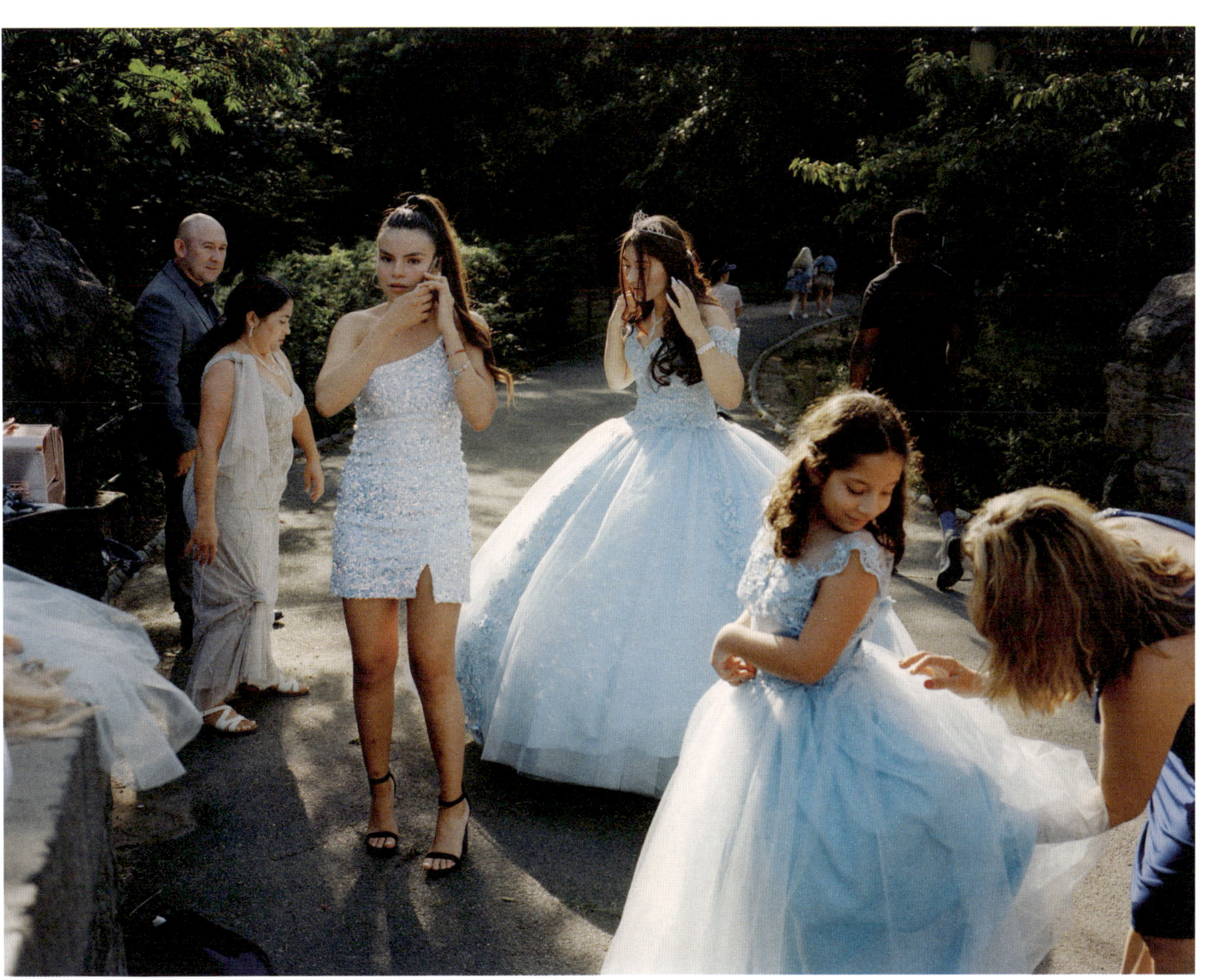

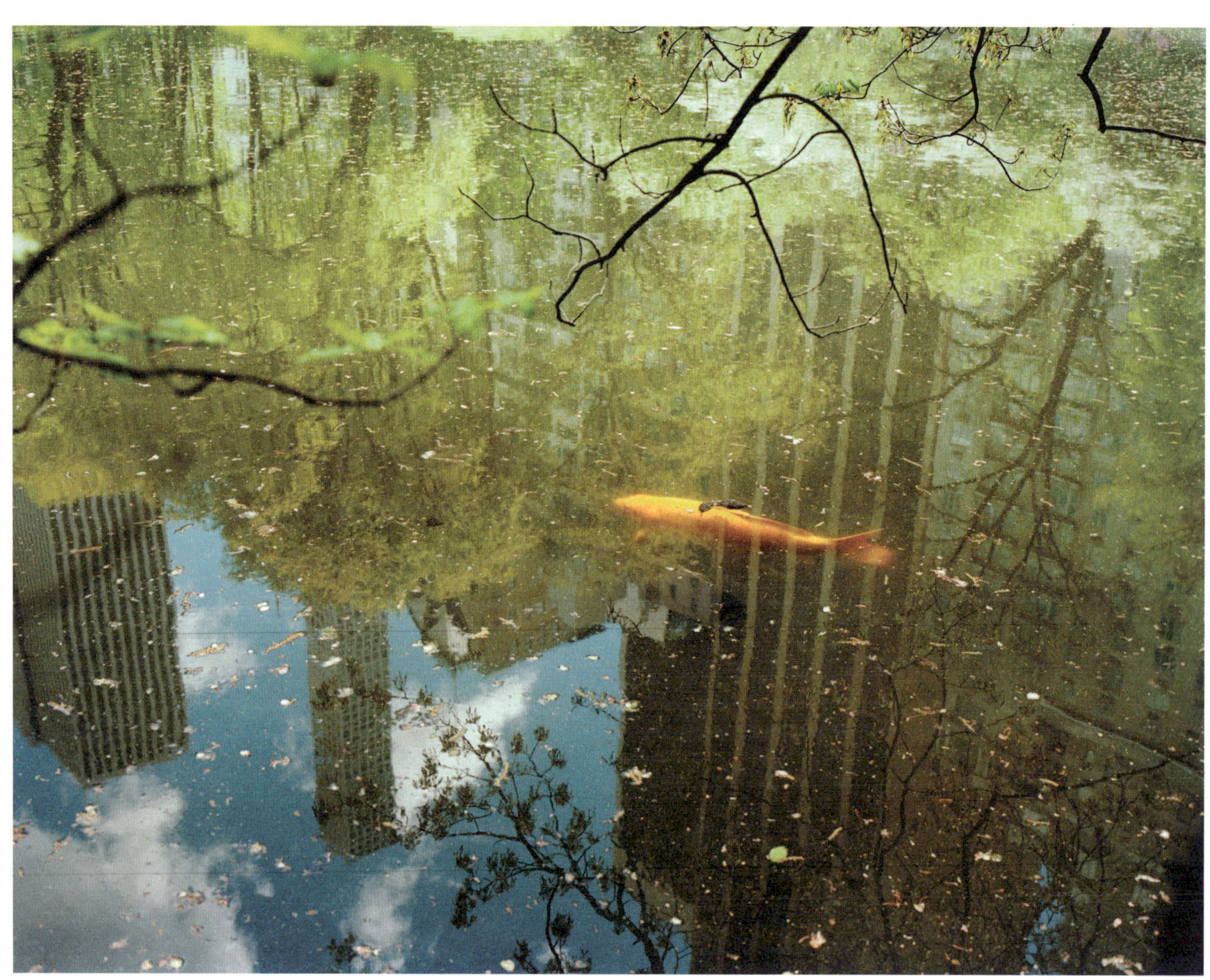

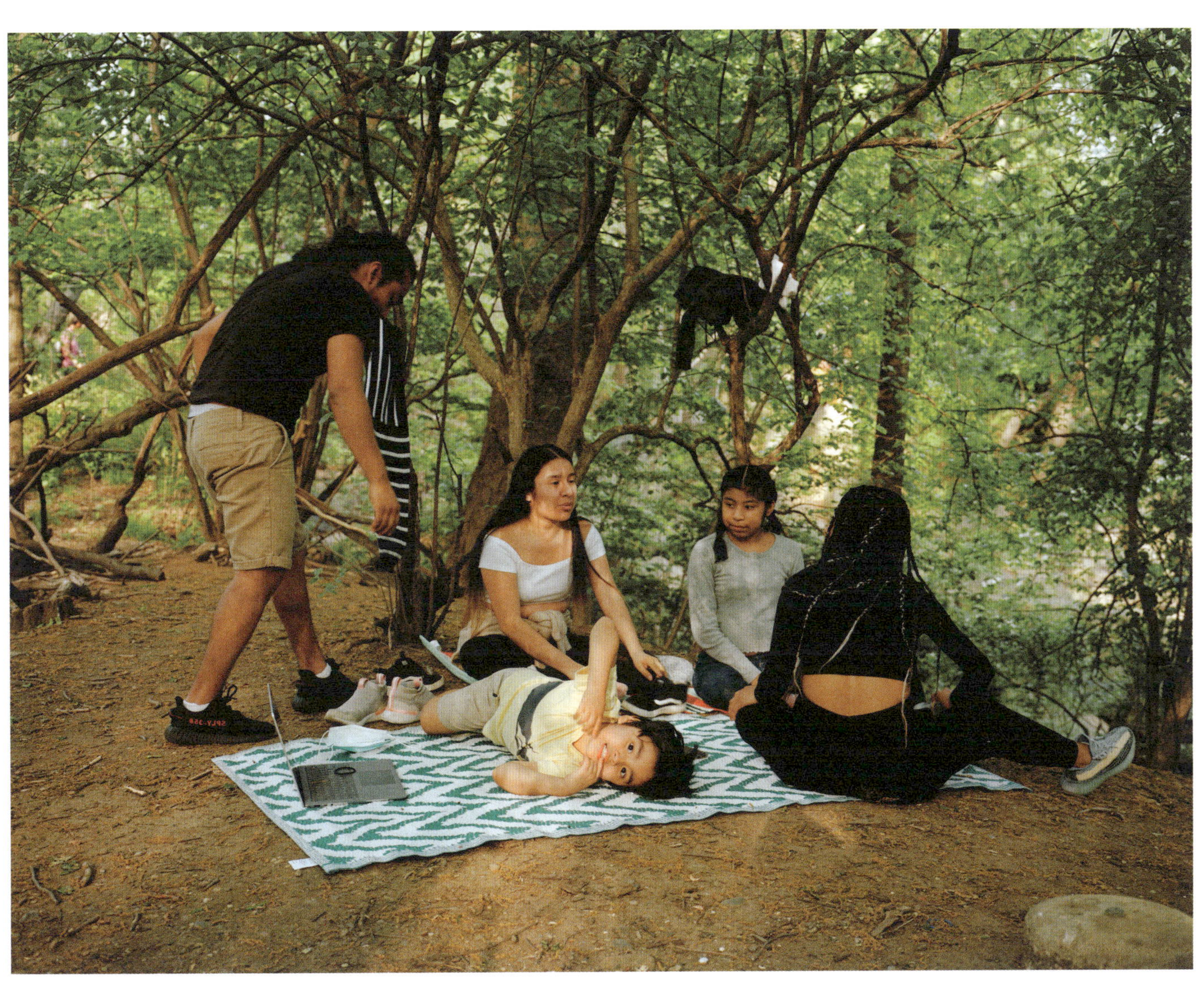

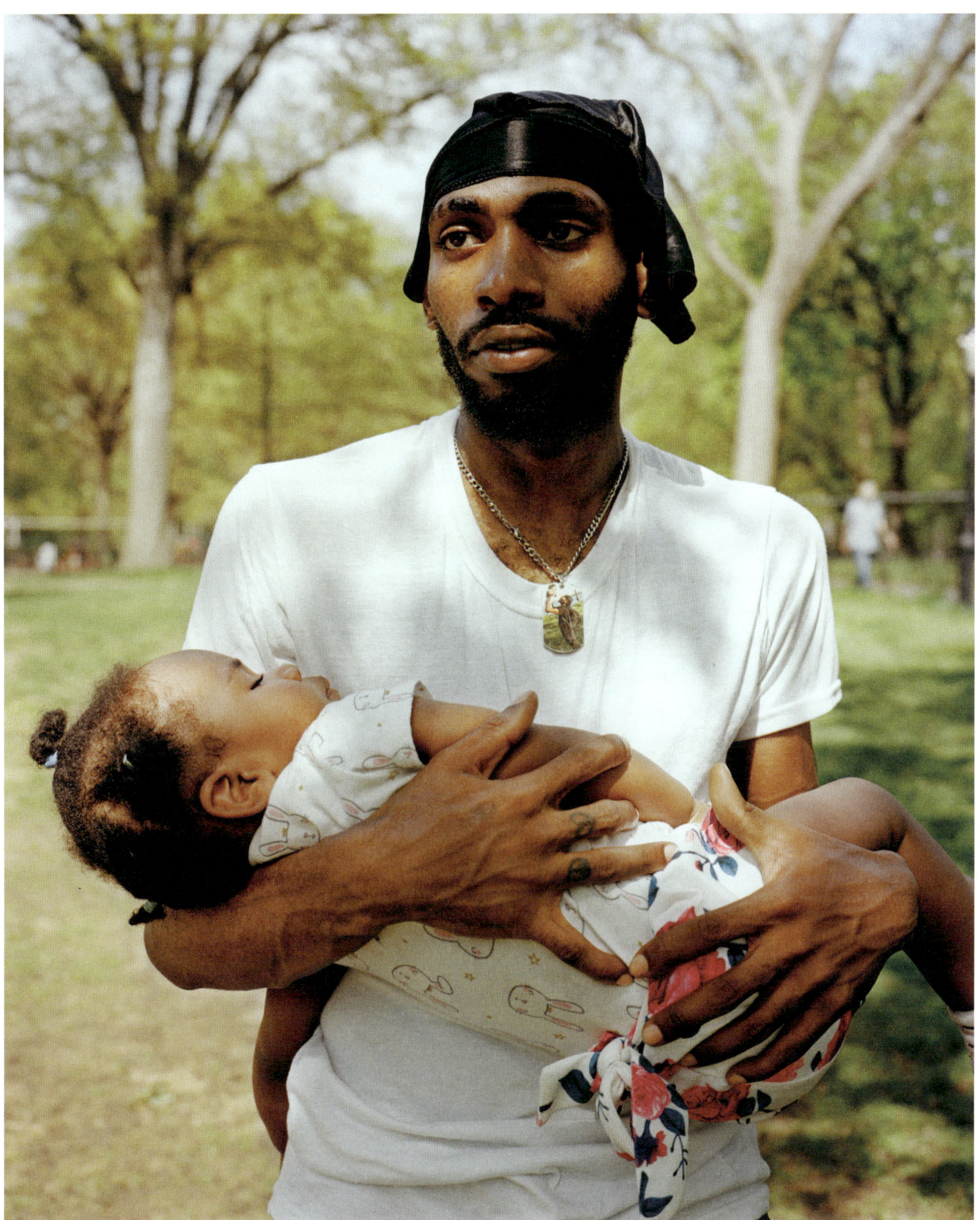

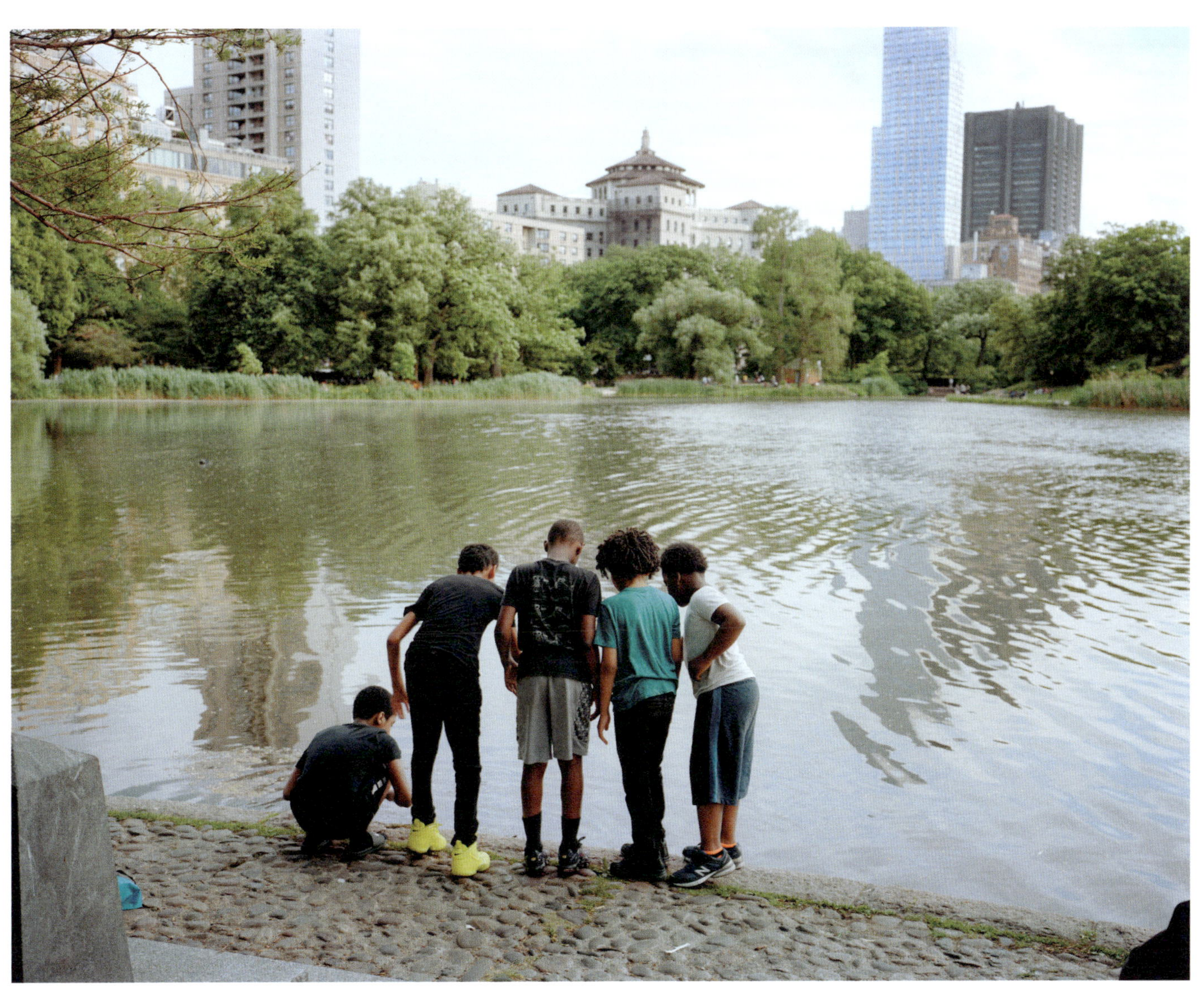

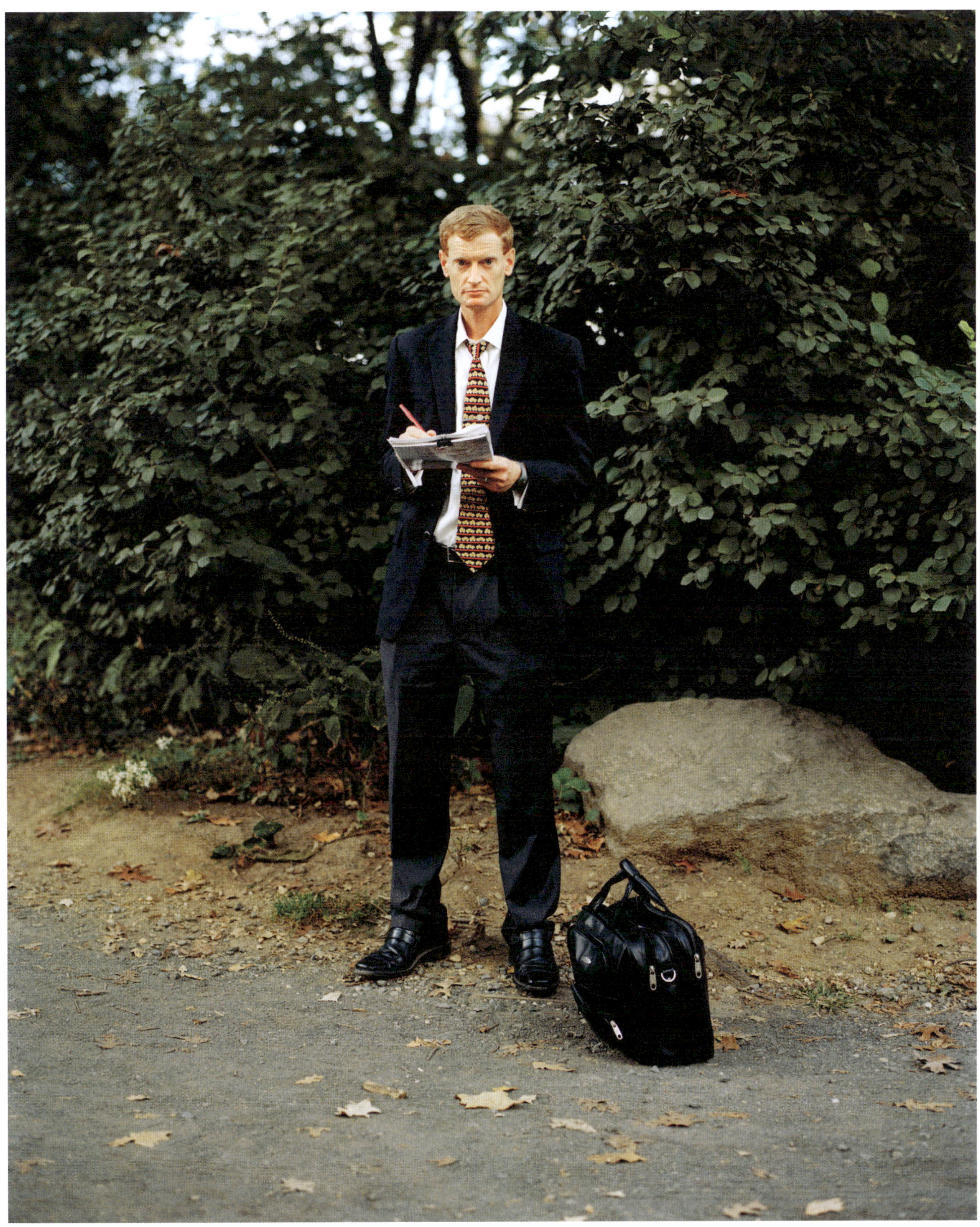

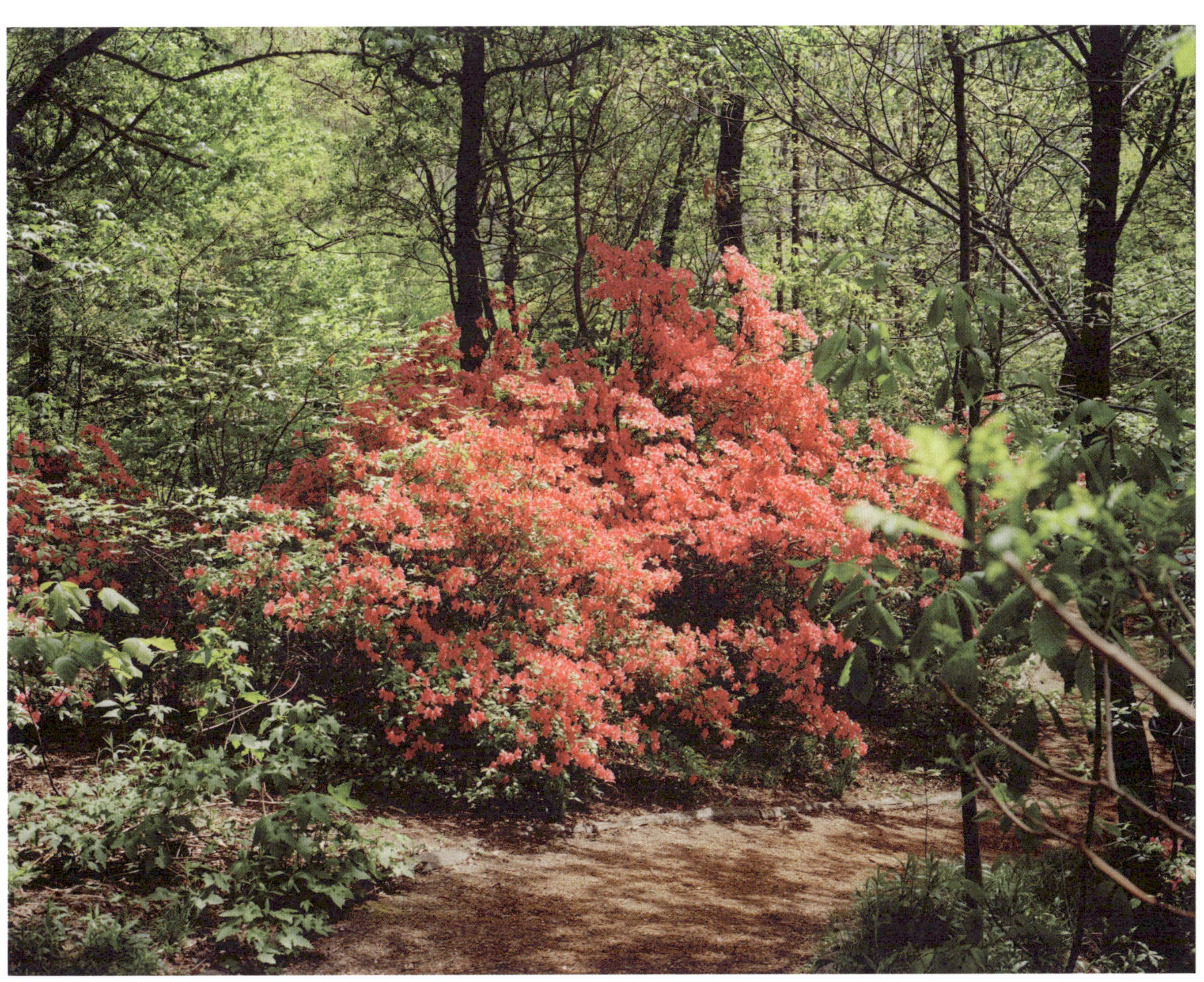

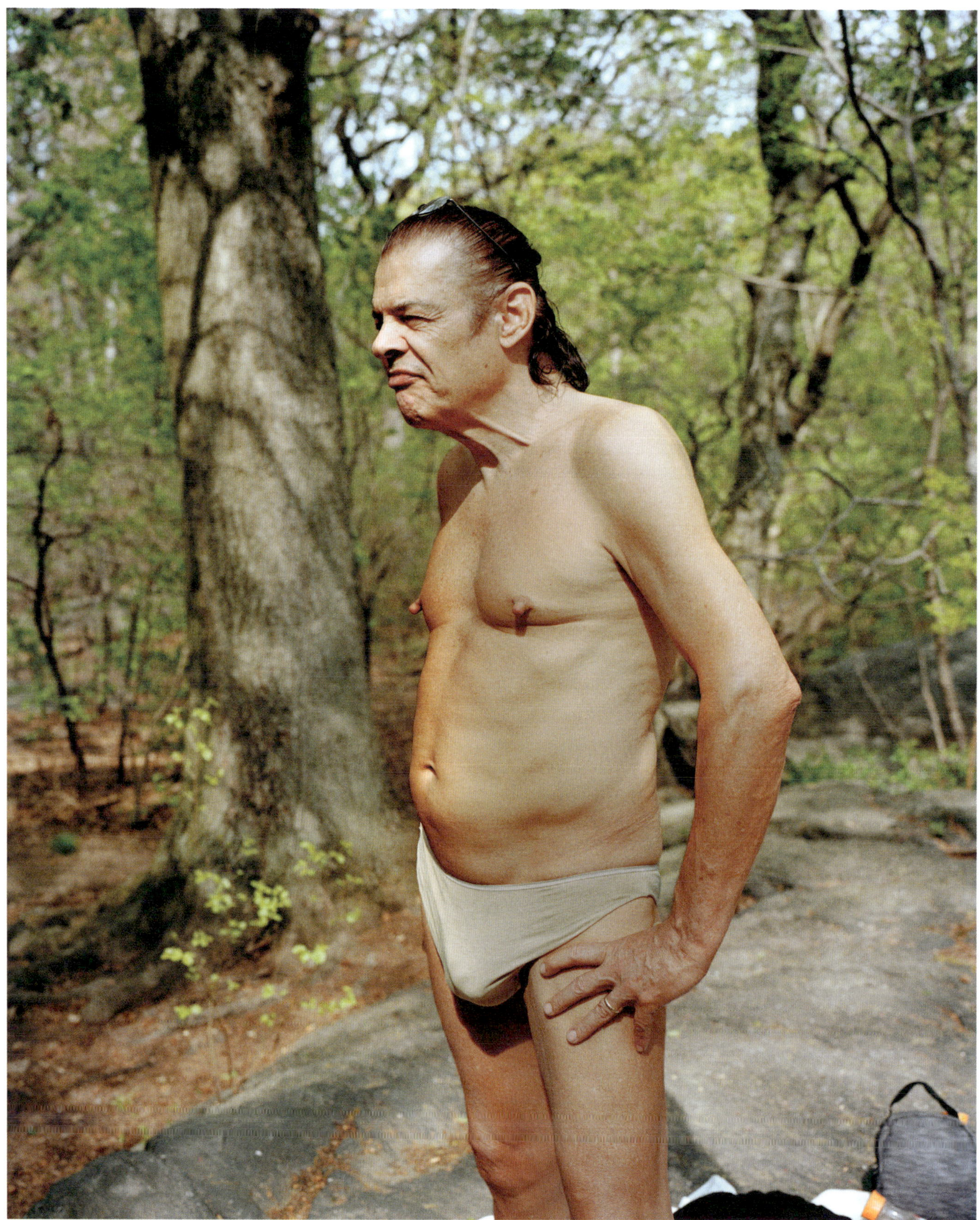

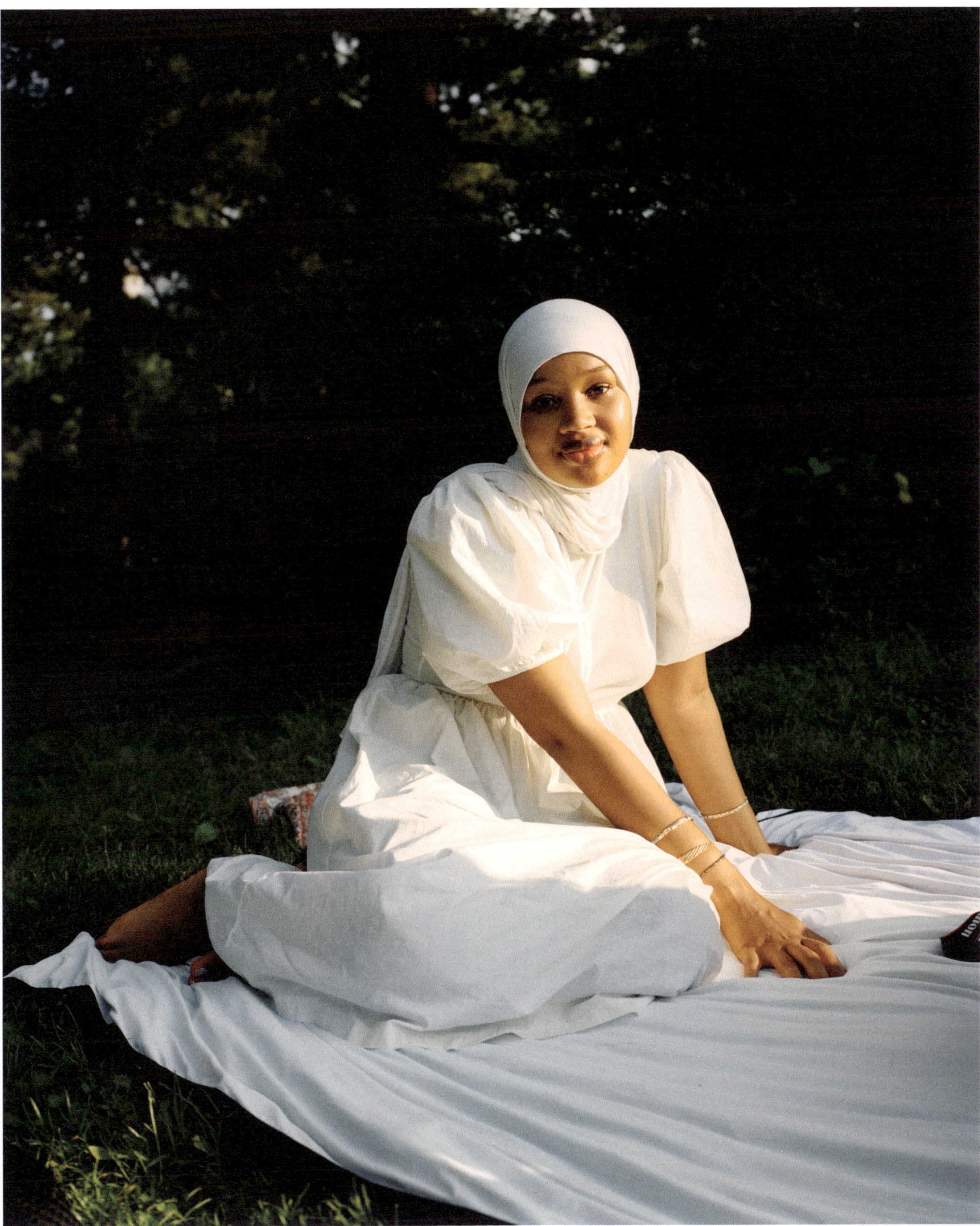

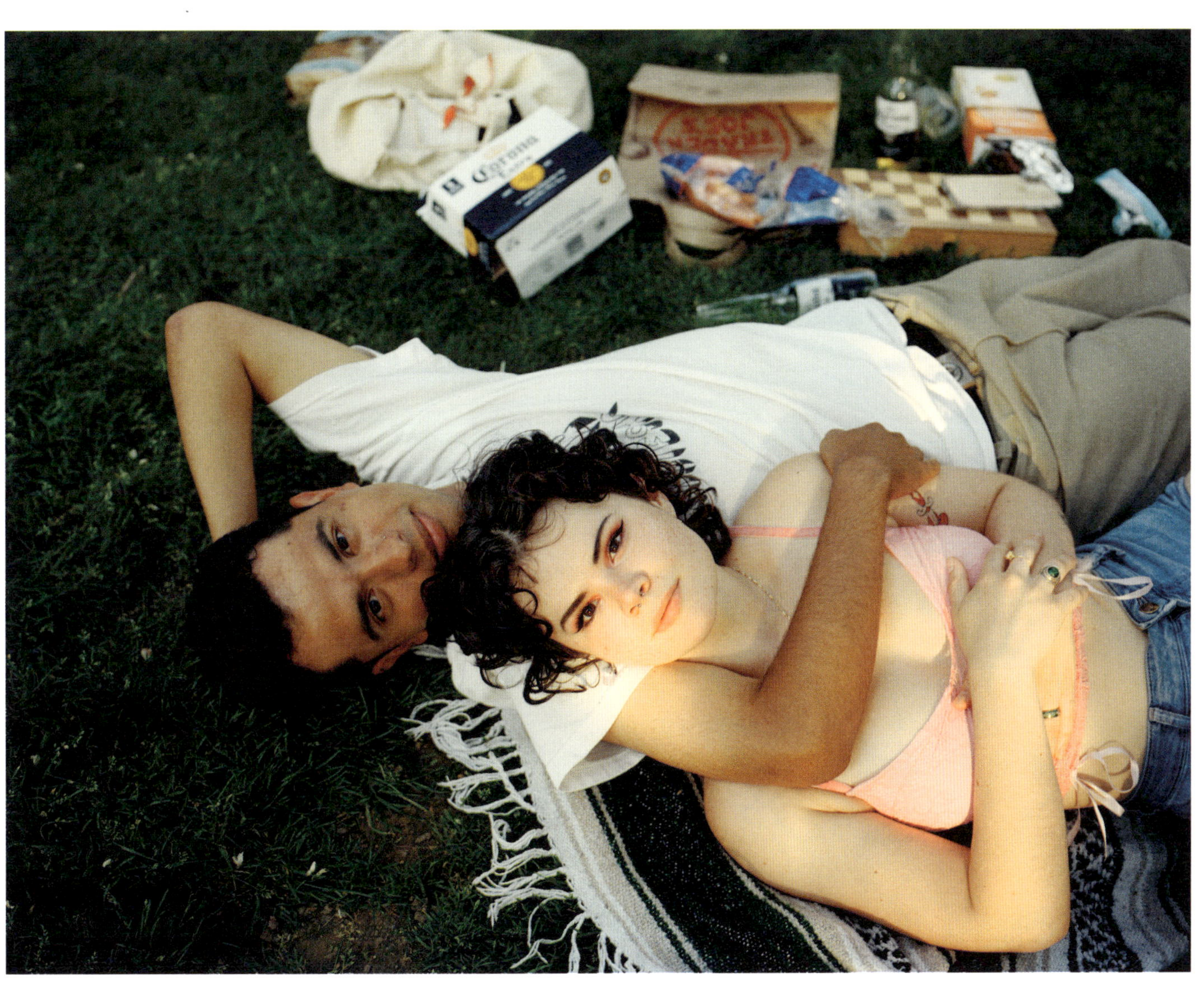
Corona

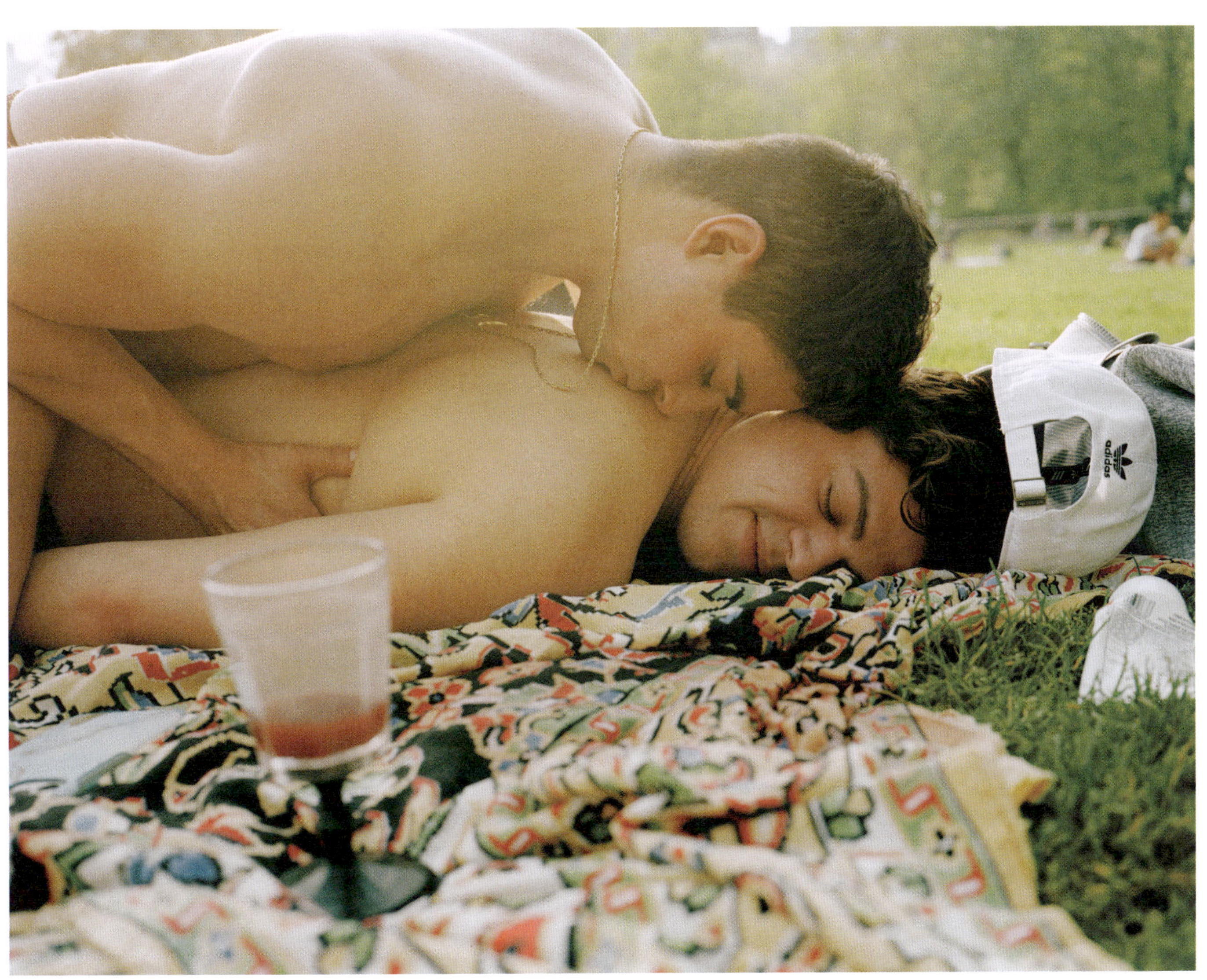
adidas

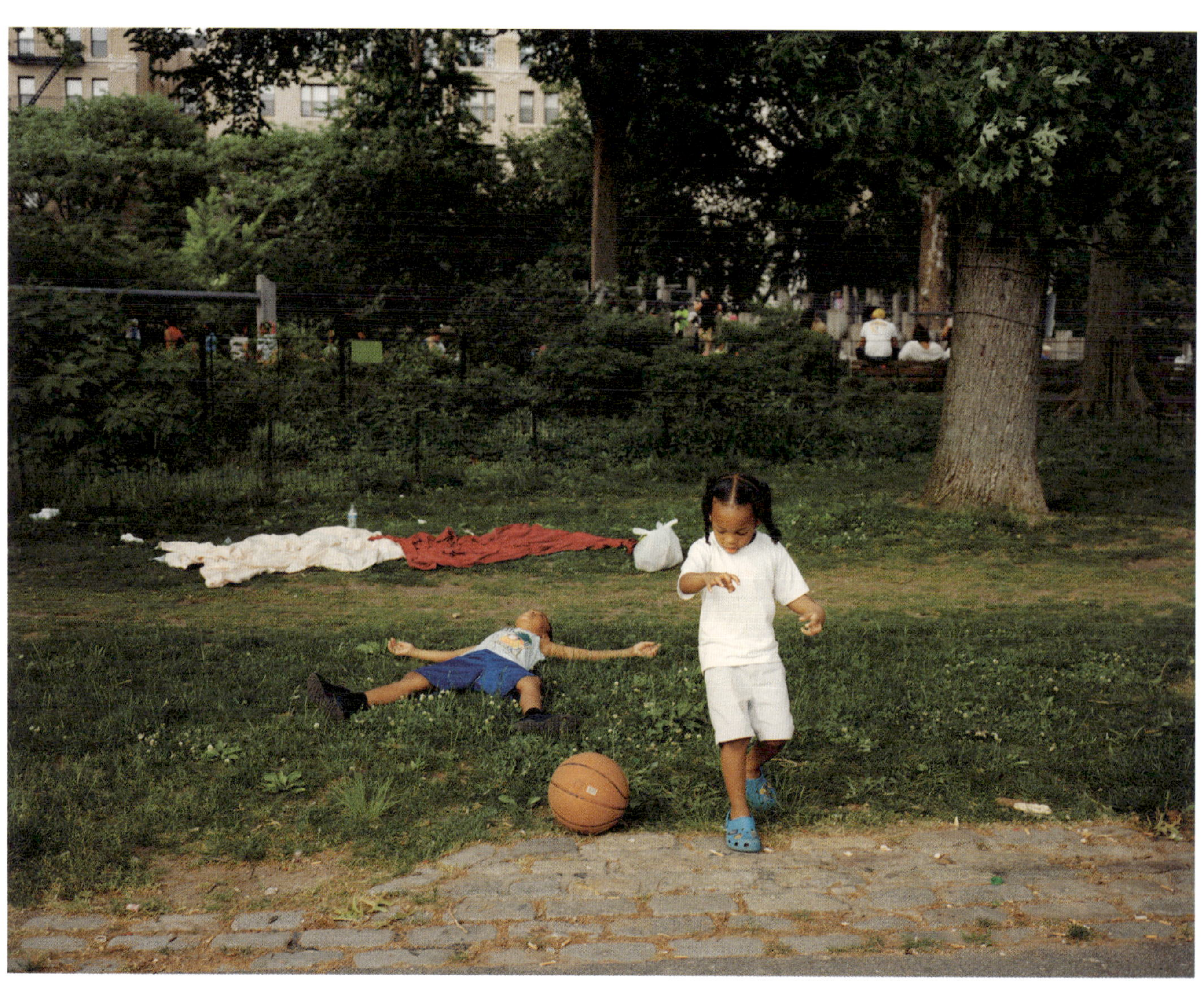

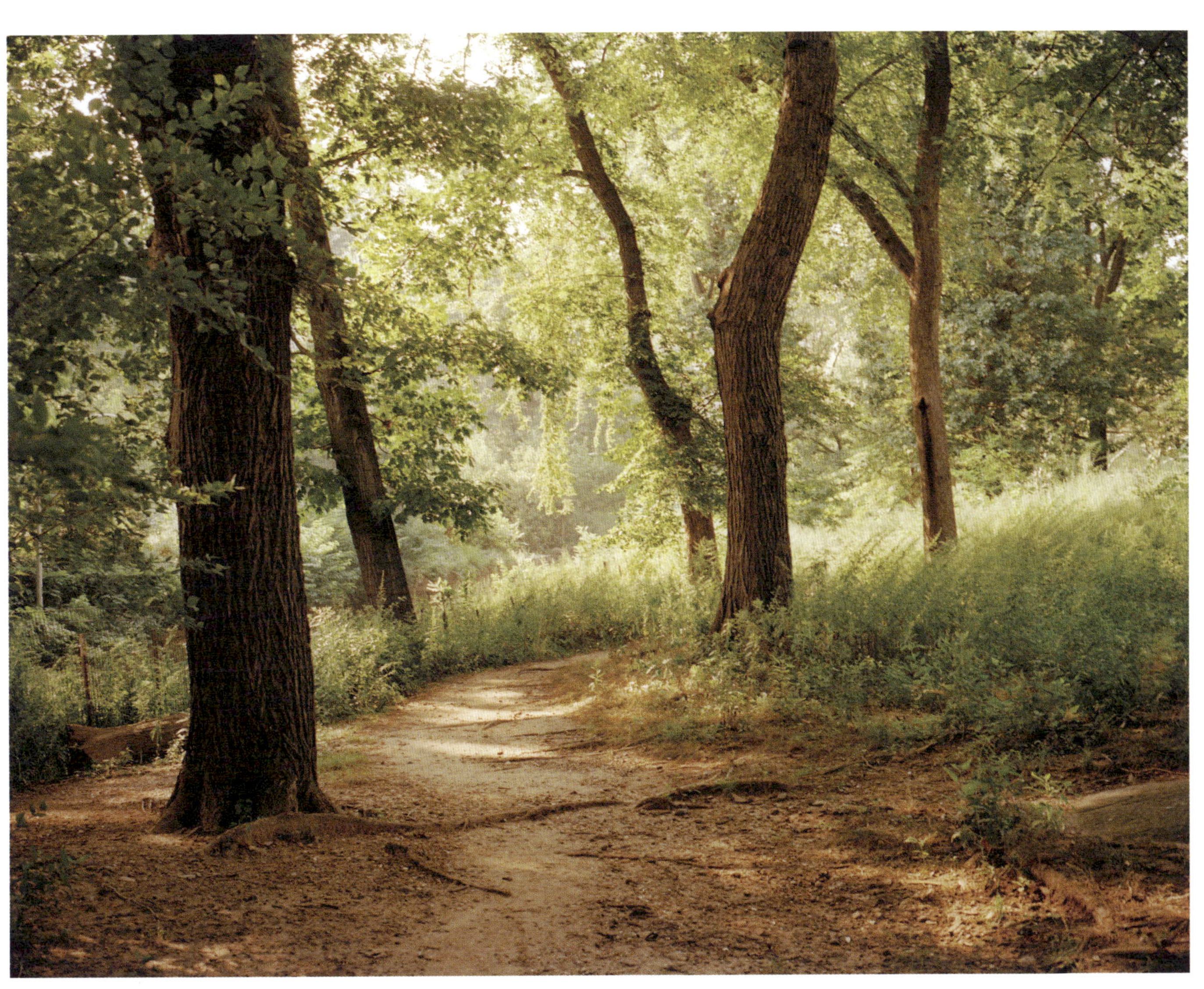

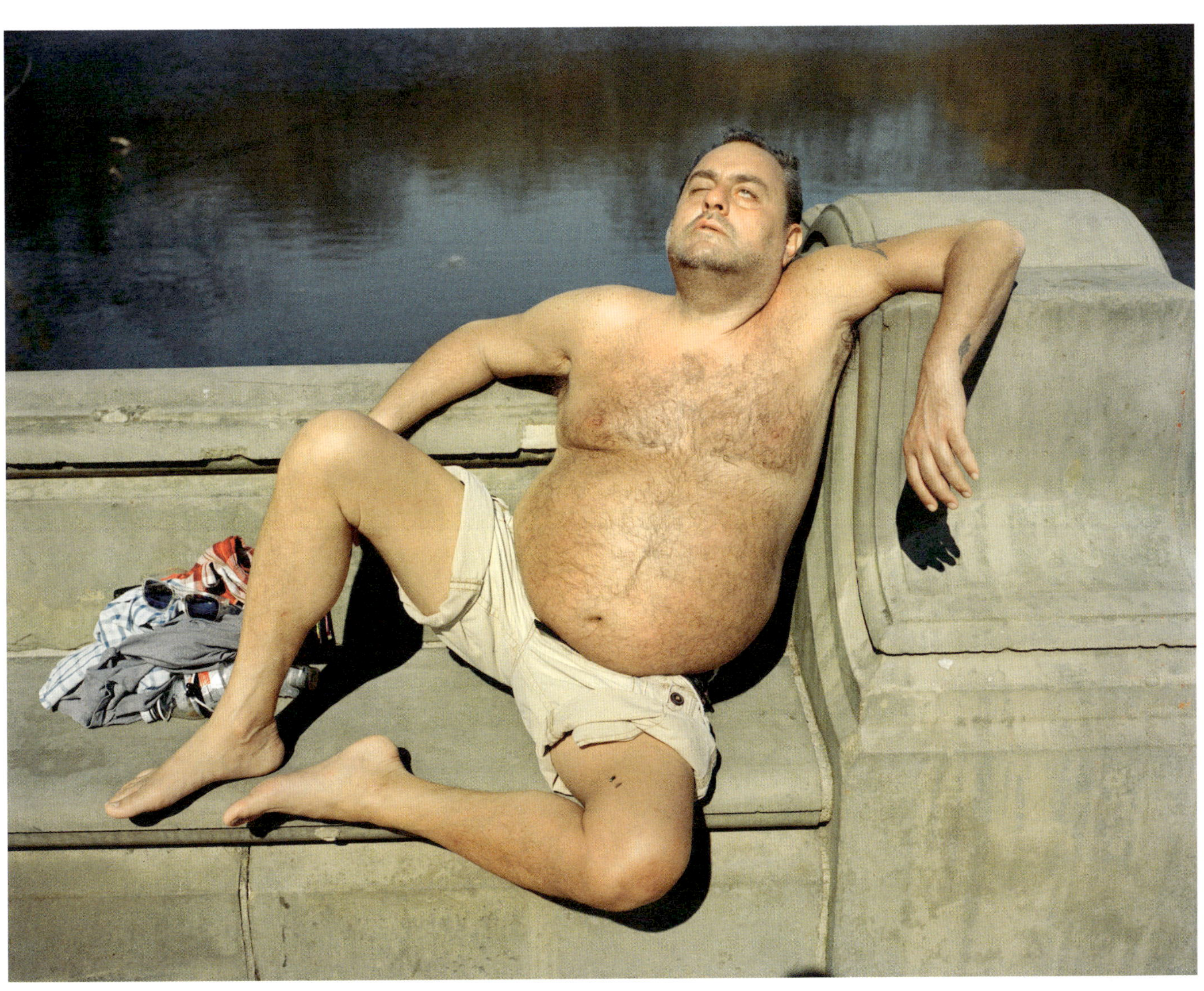

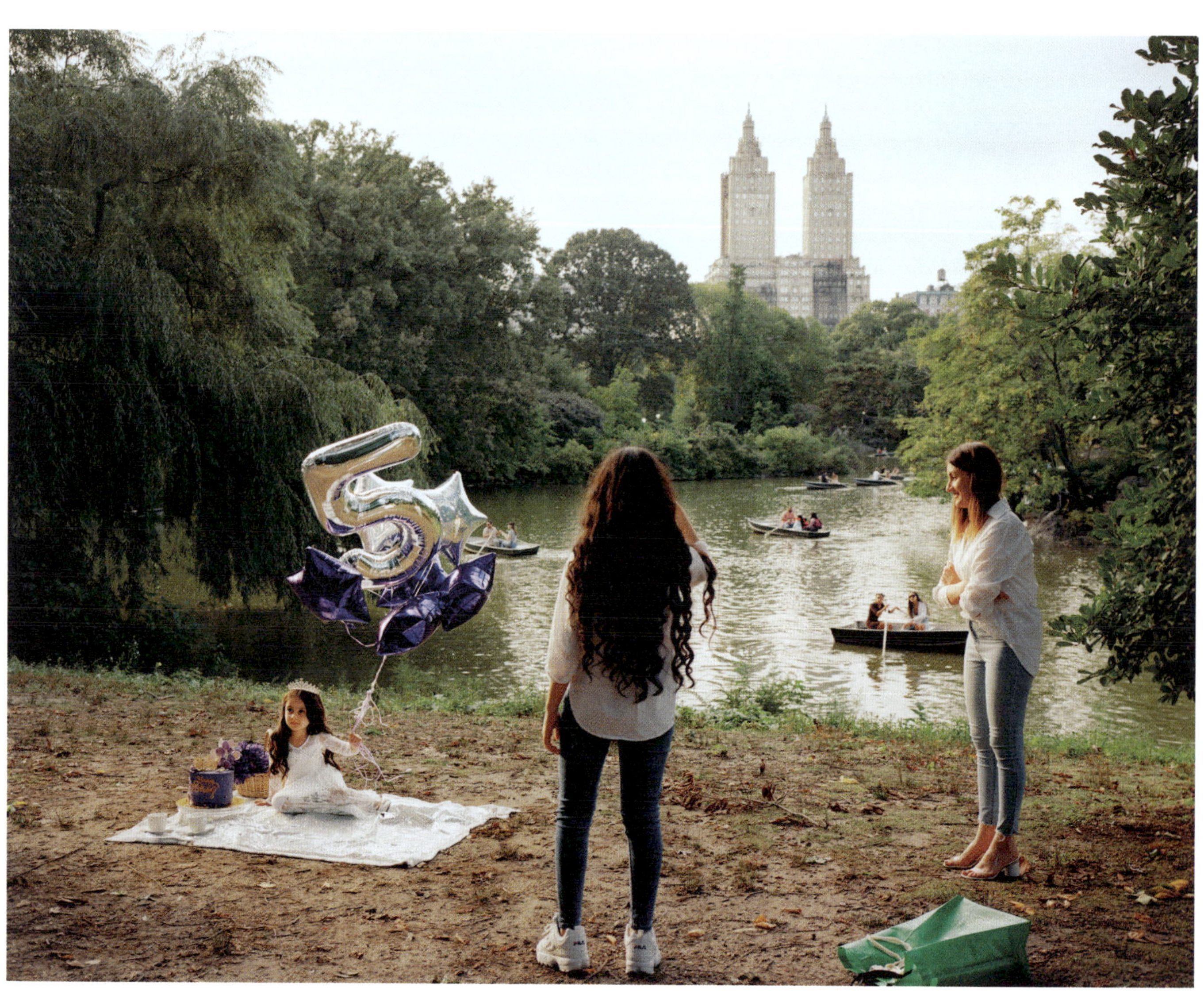

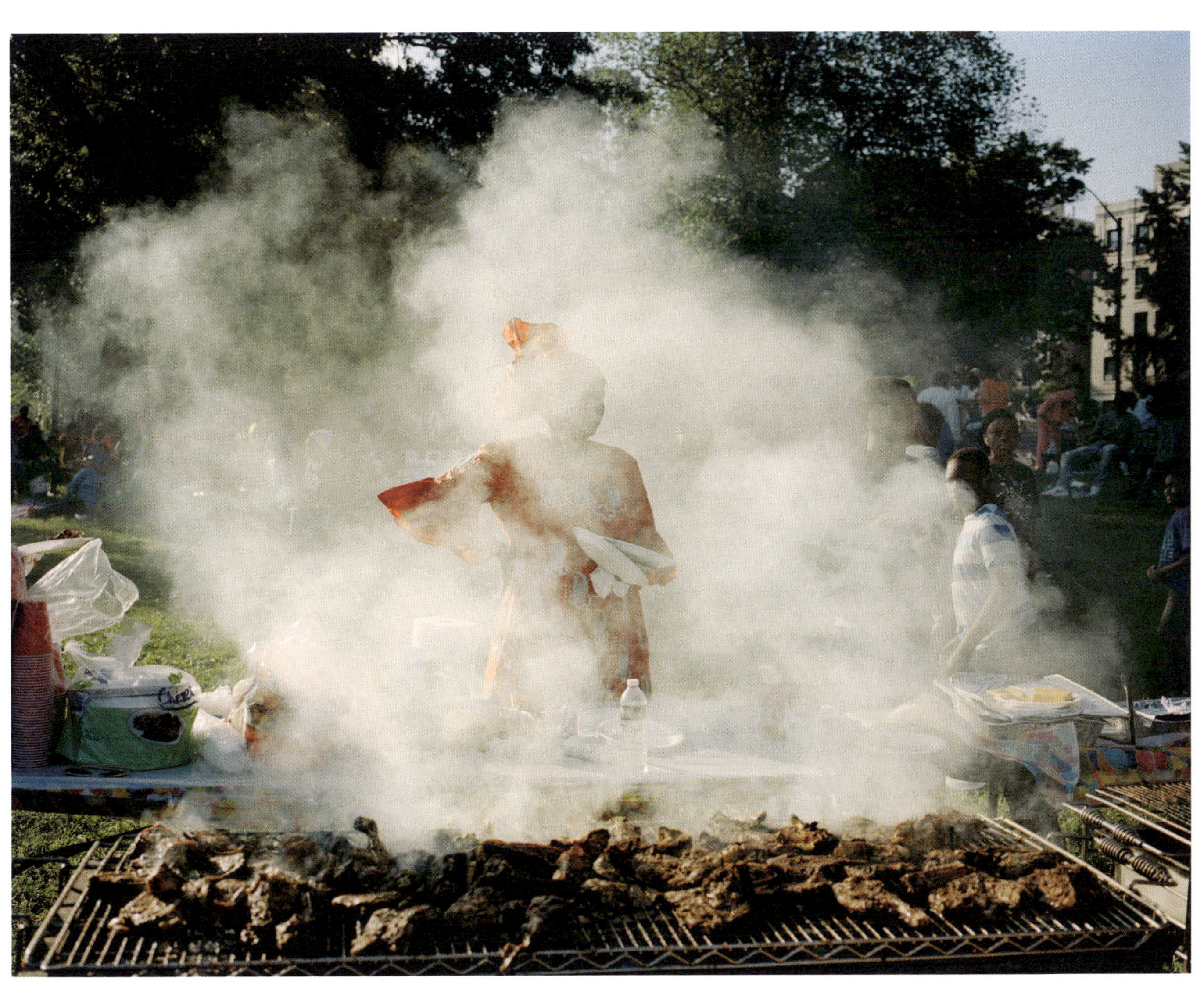

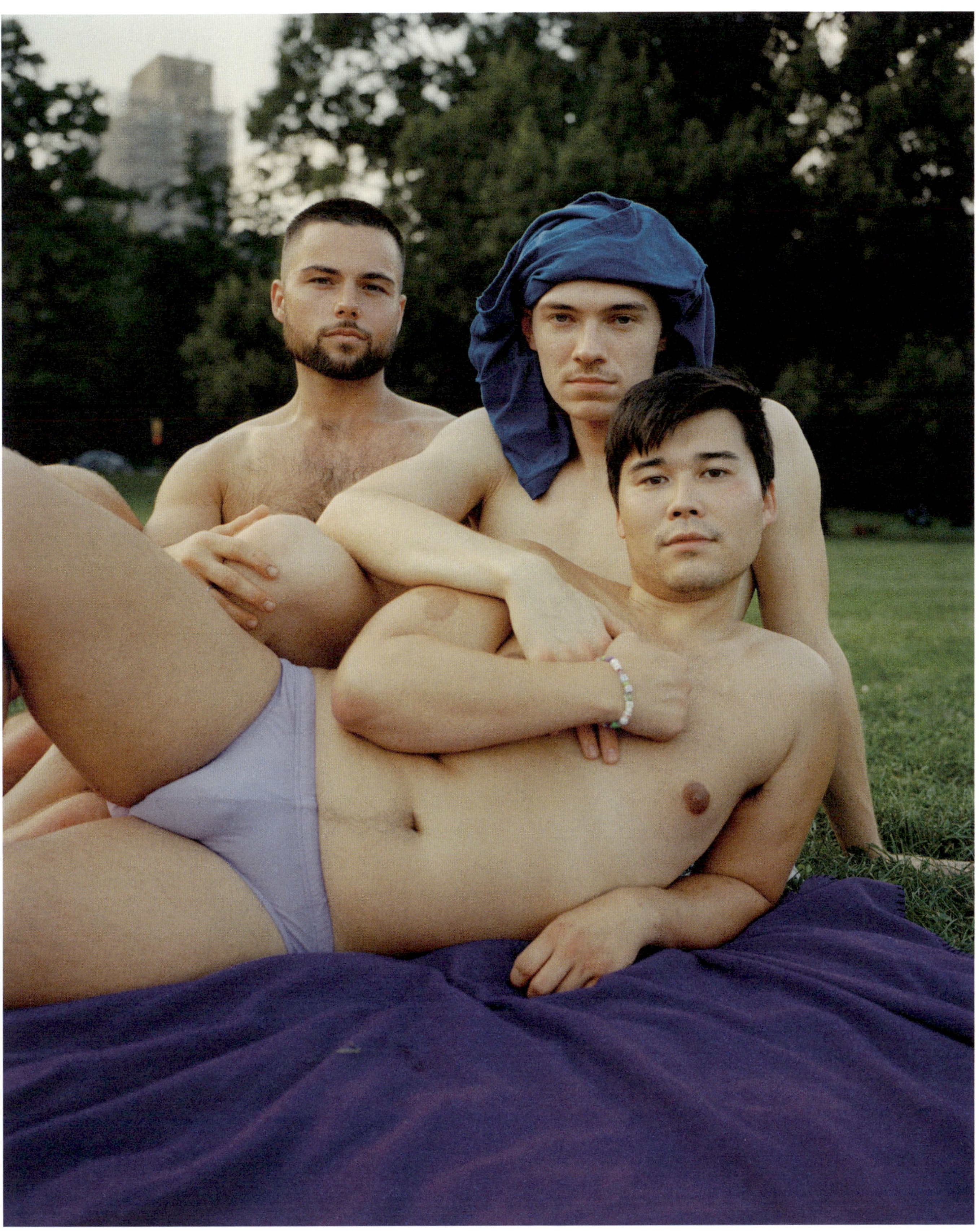

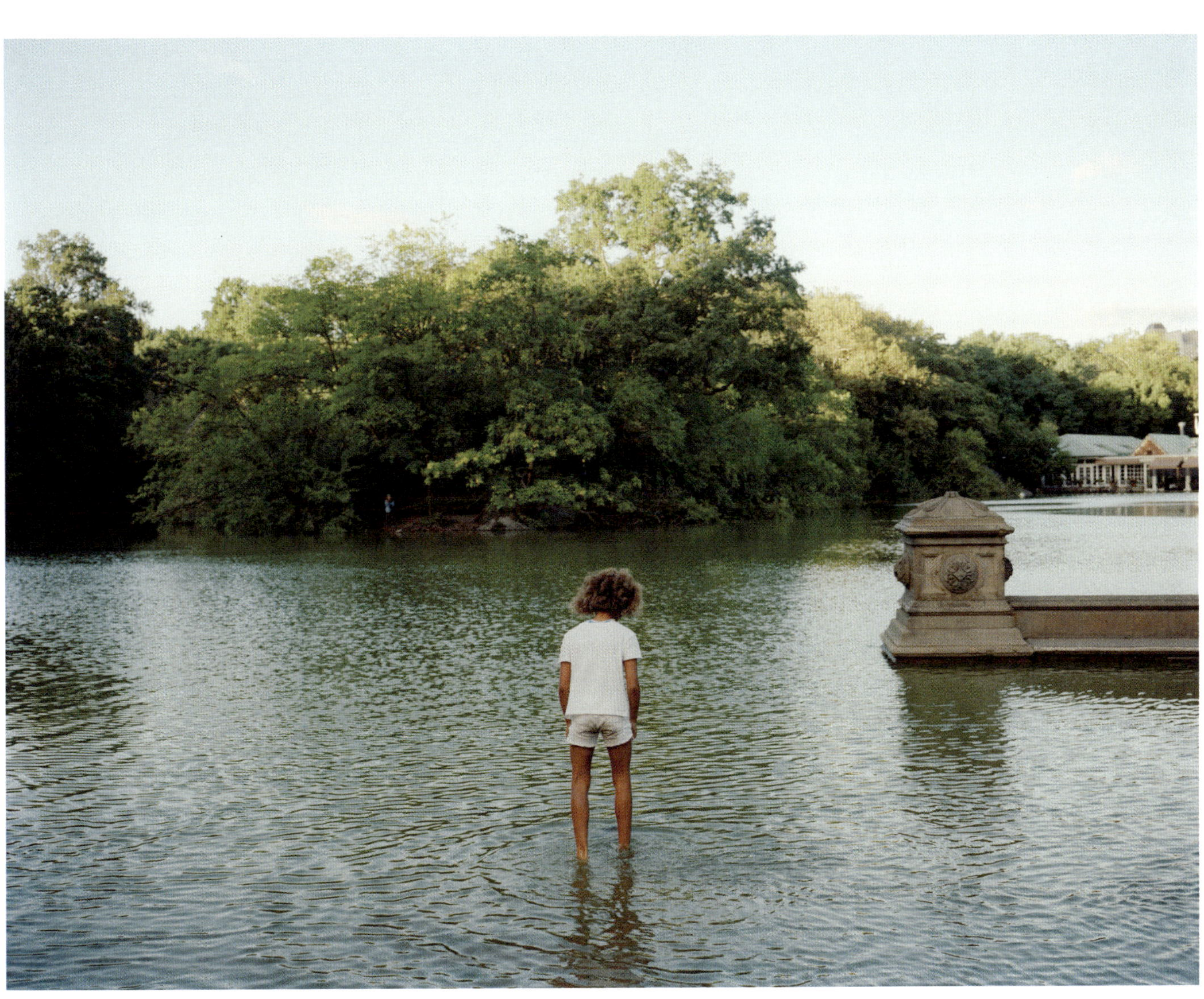

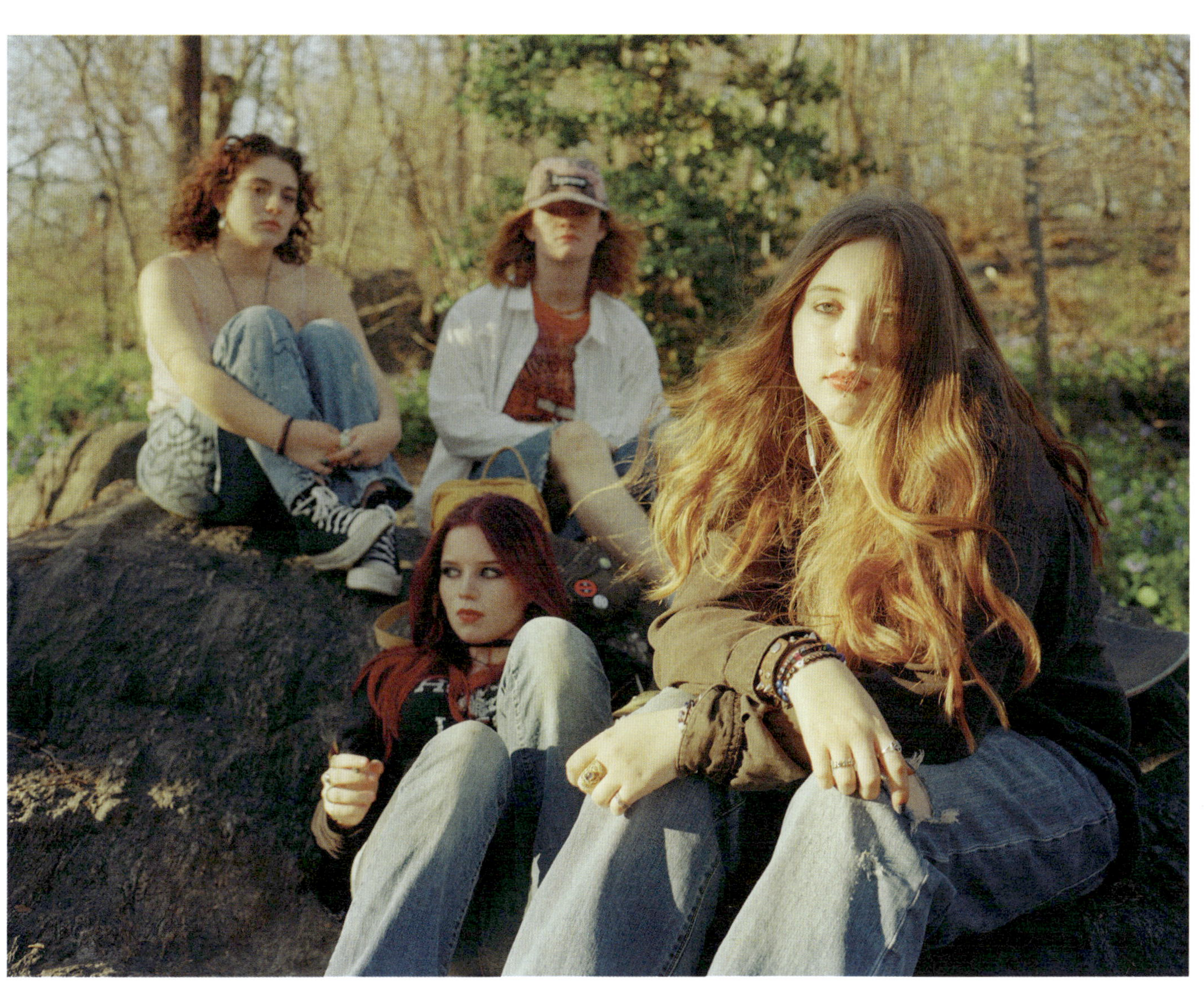

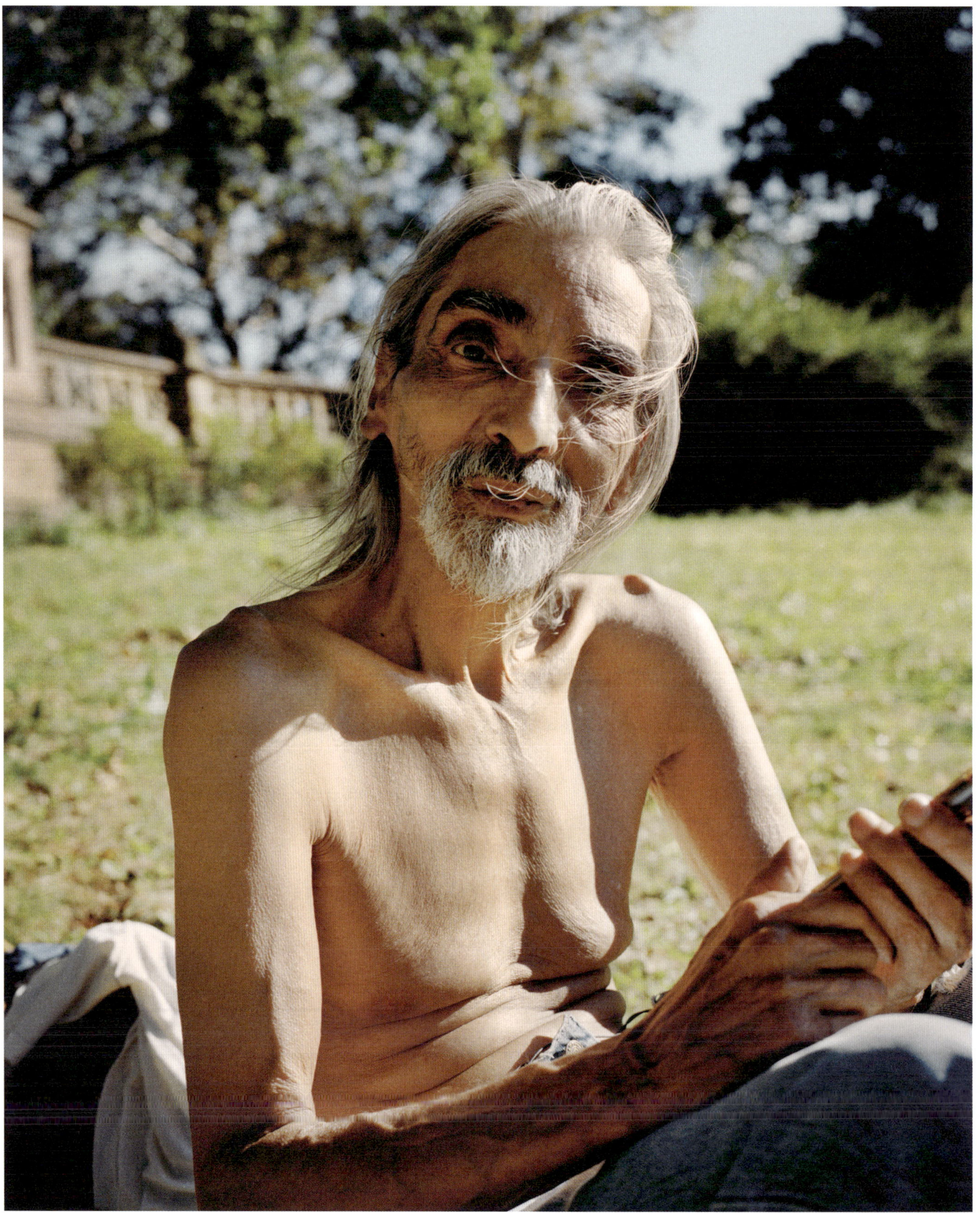

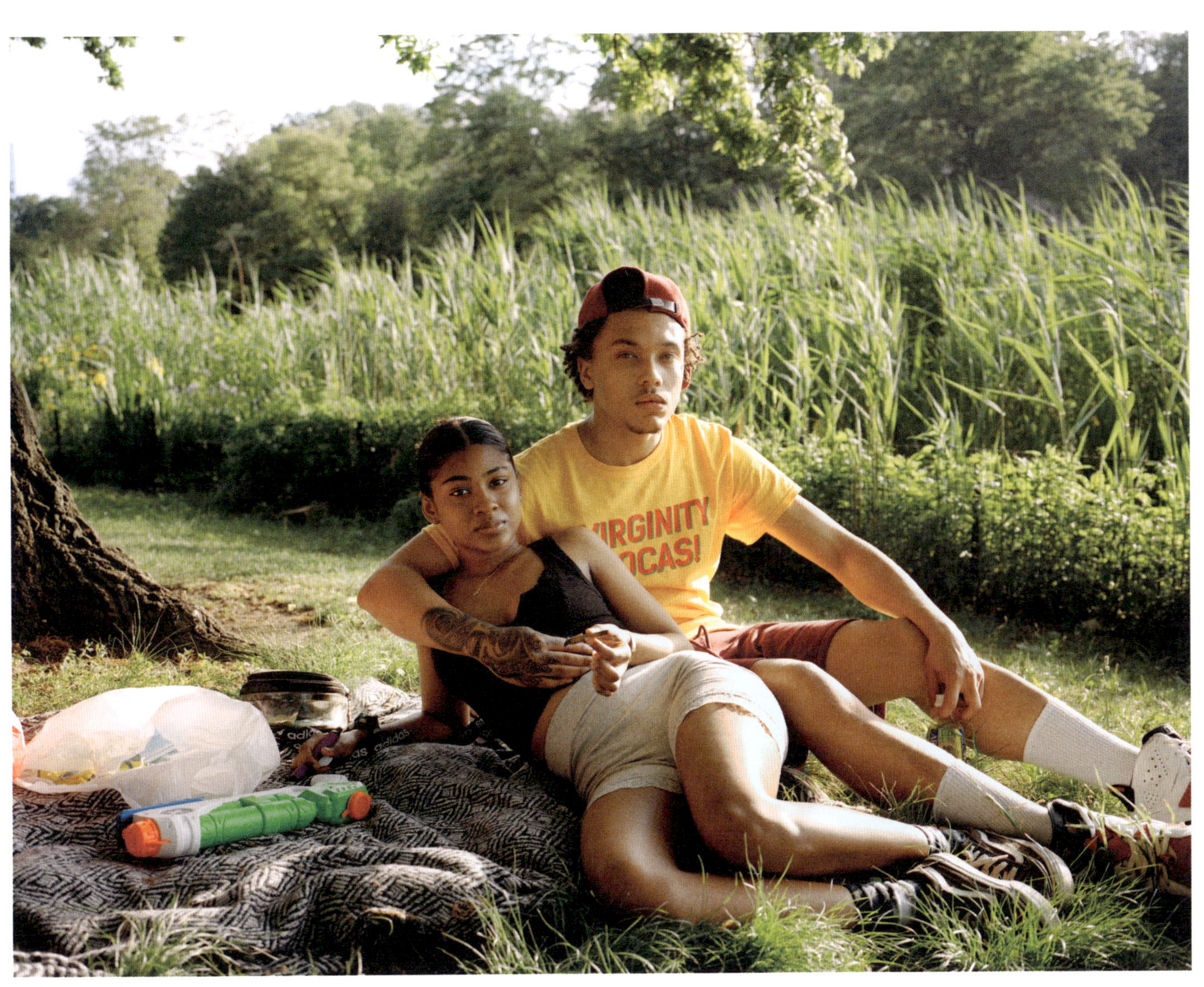
IRGINITY
OCAS!

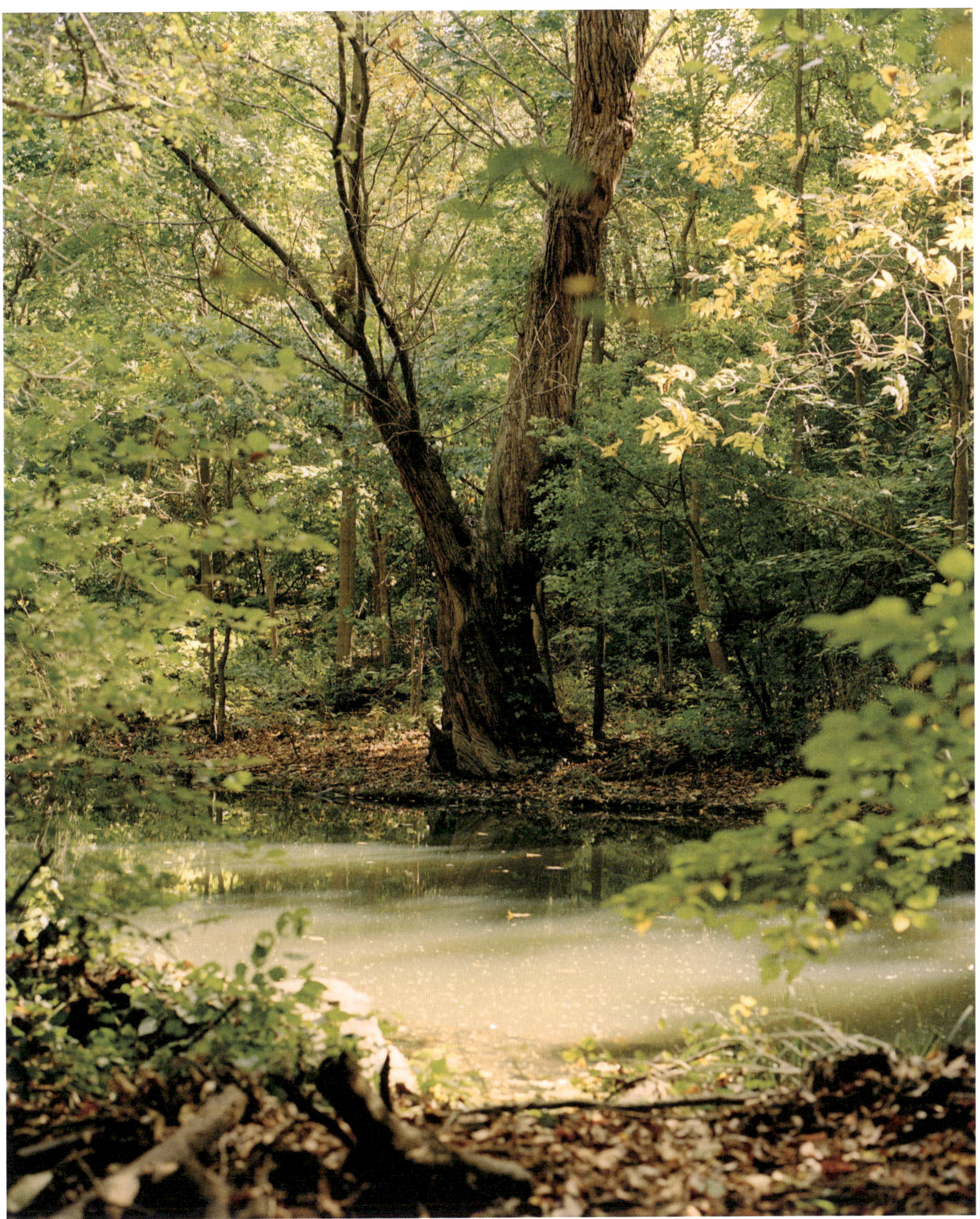

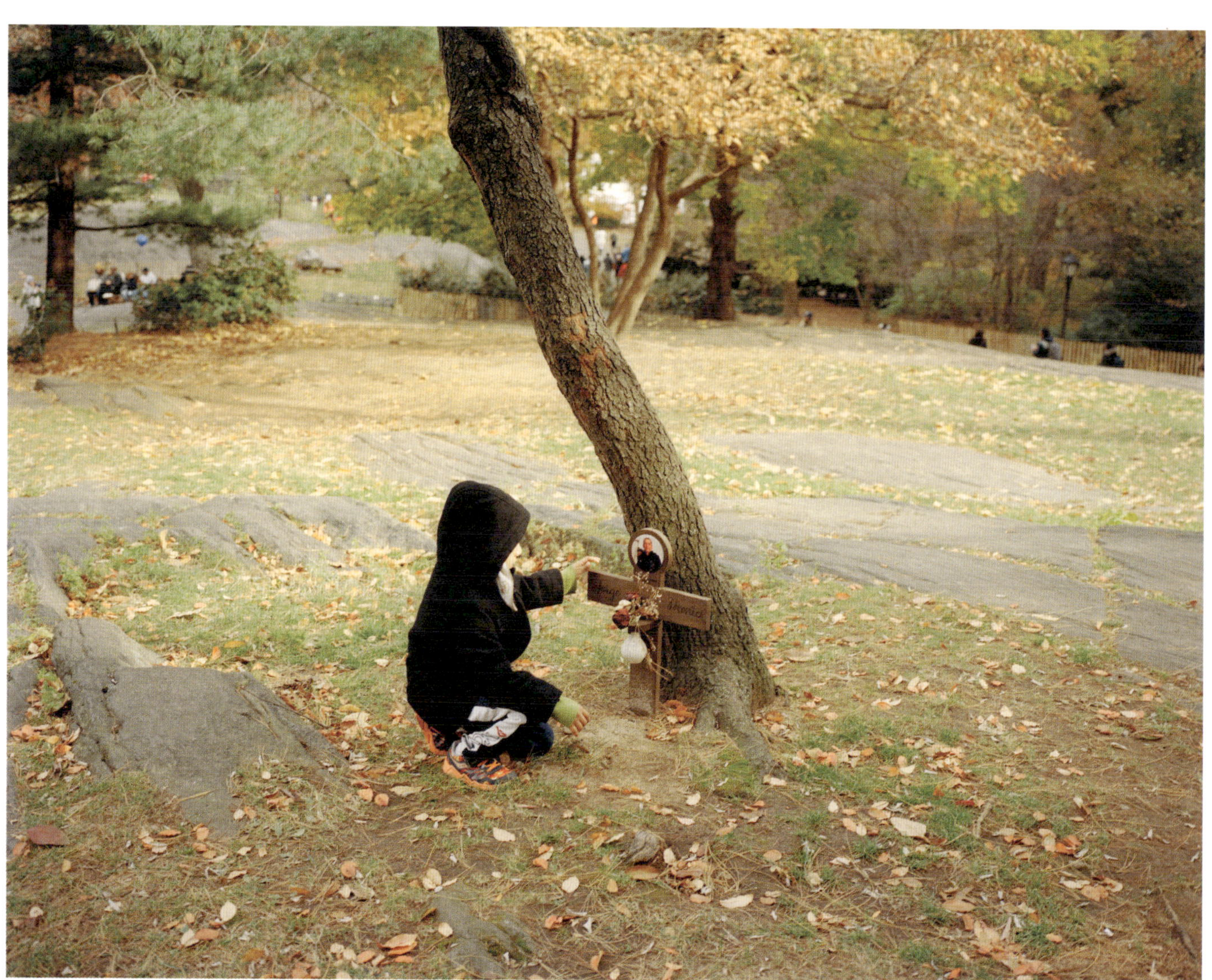

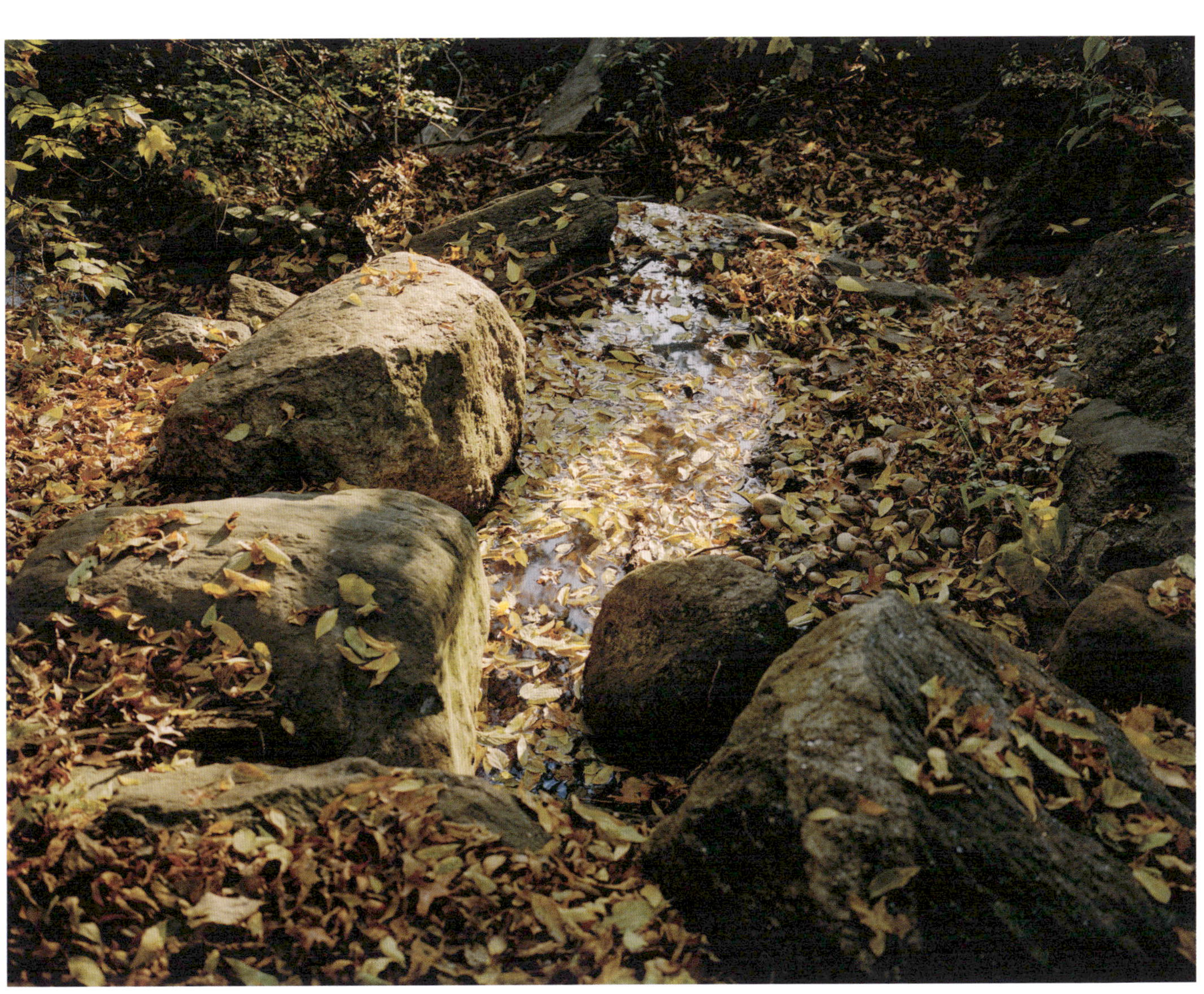

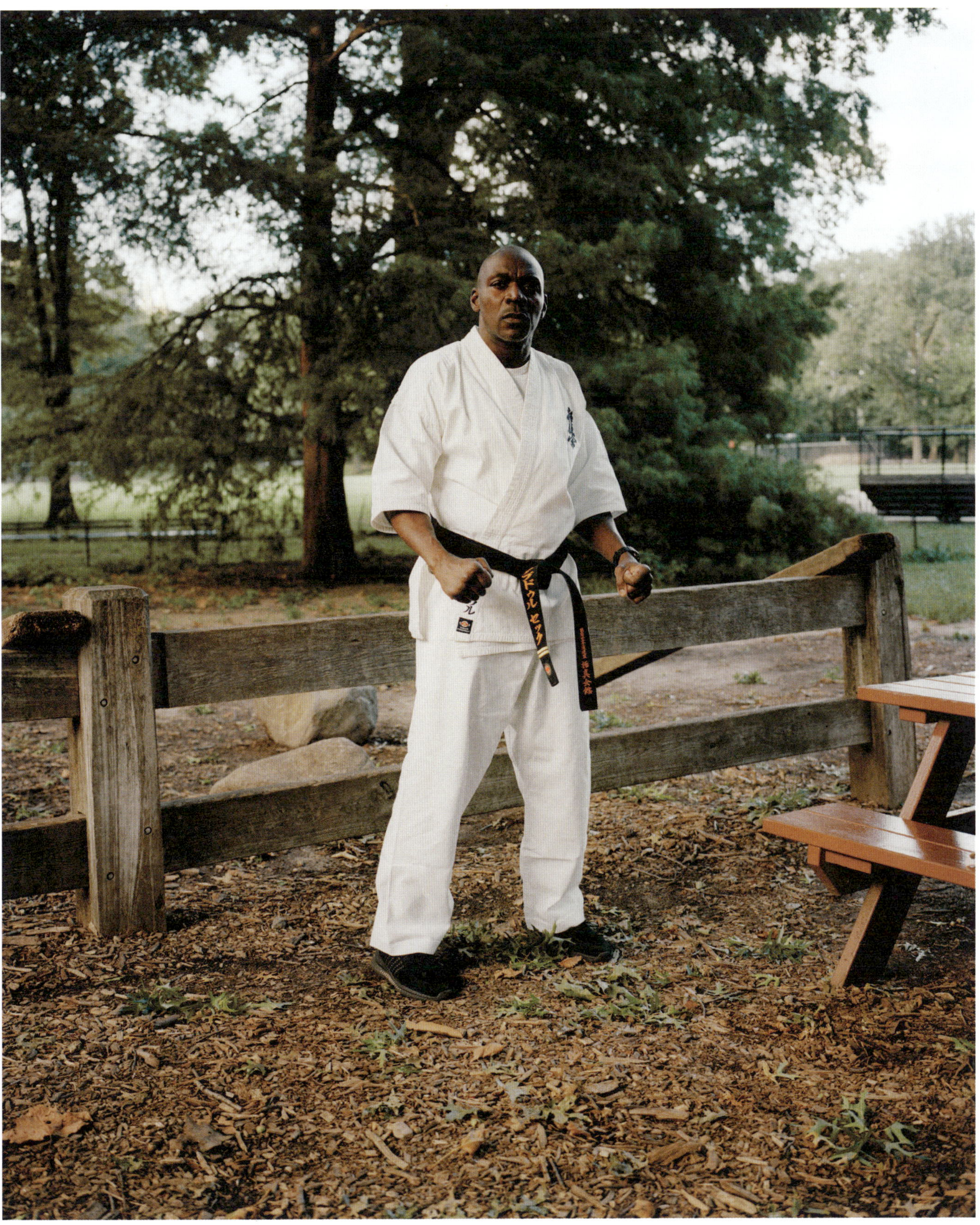

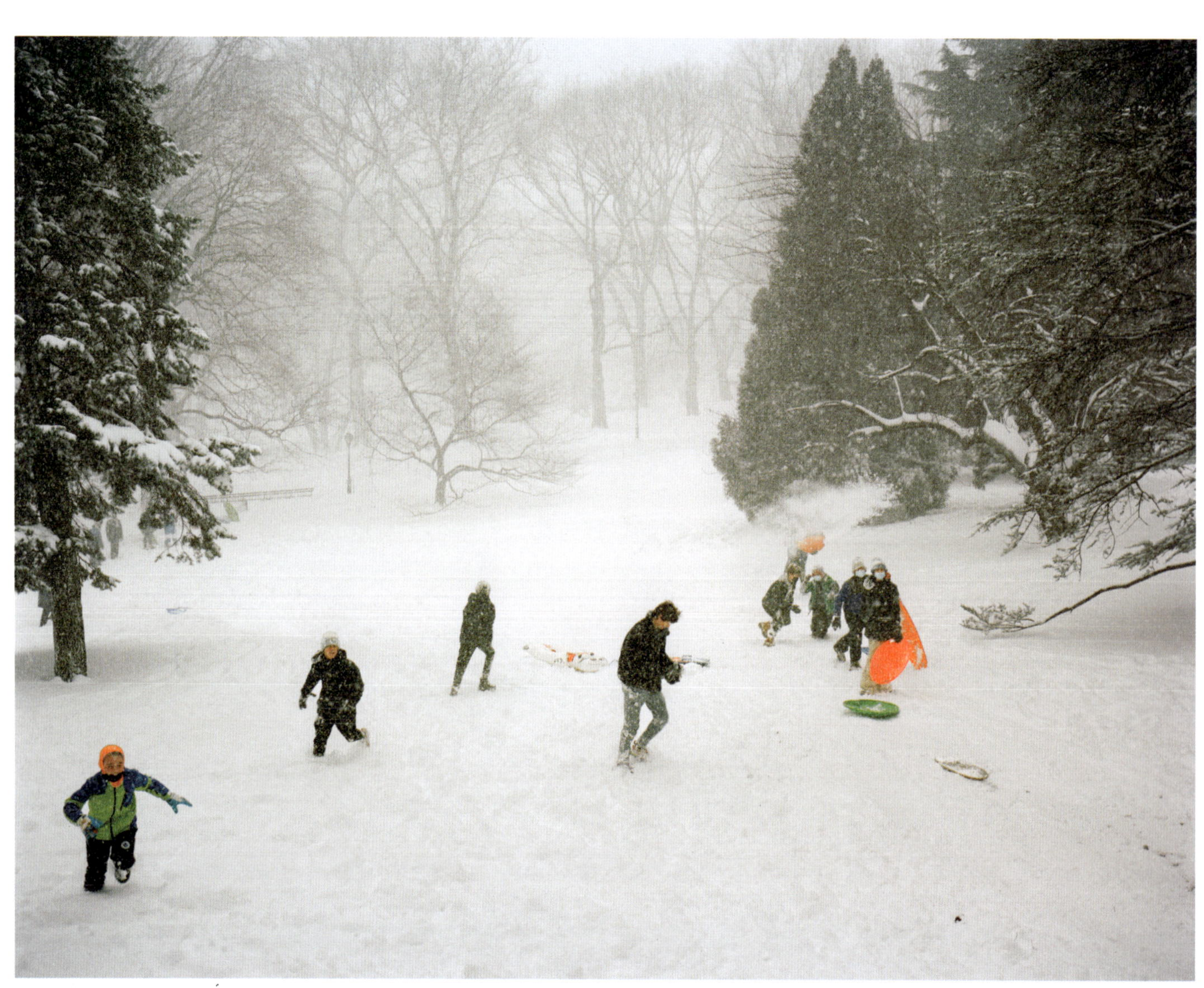

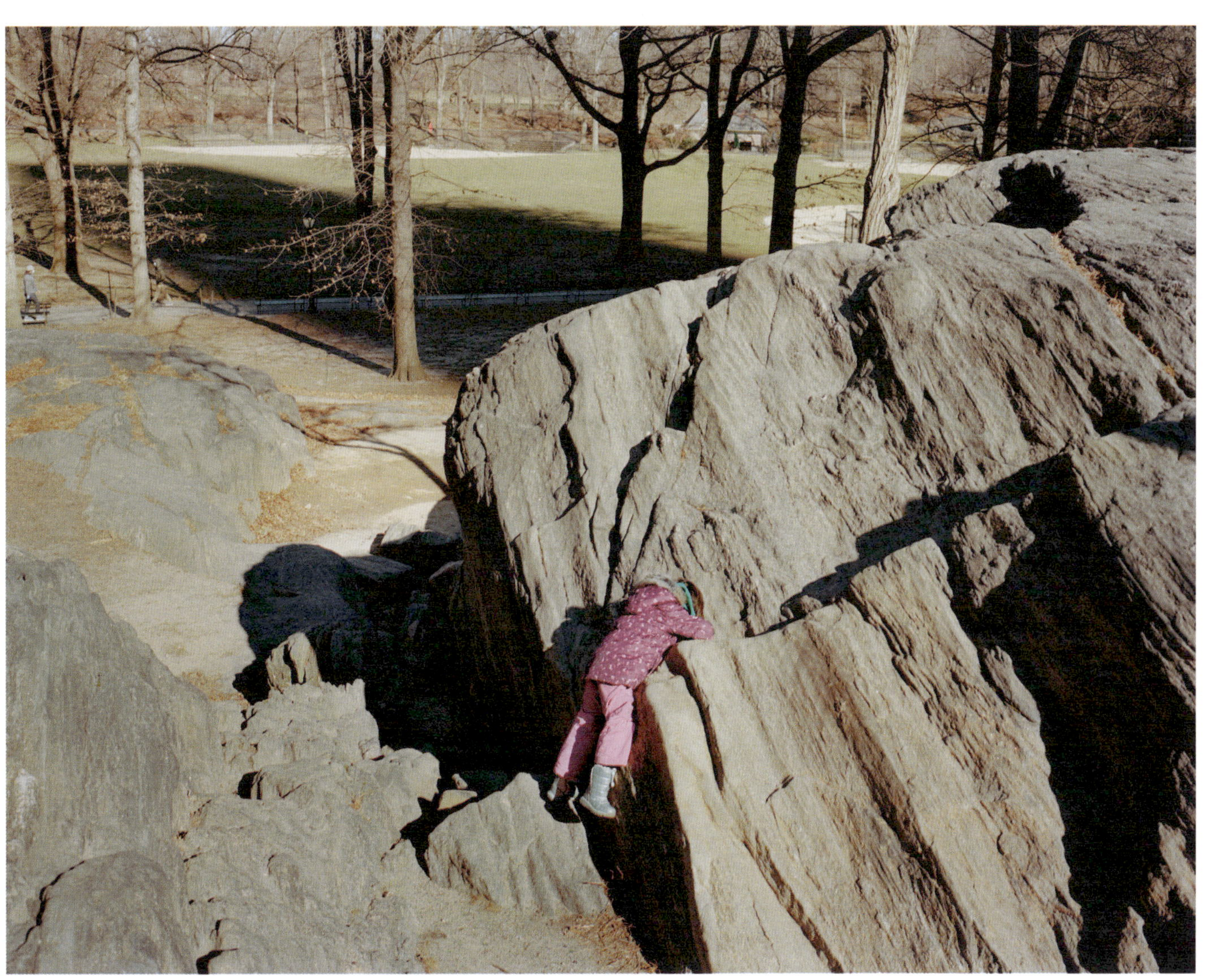

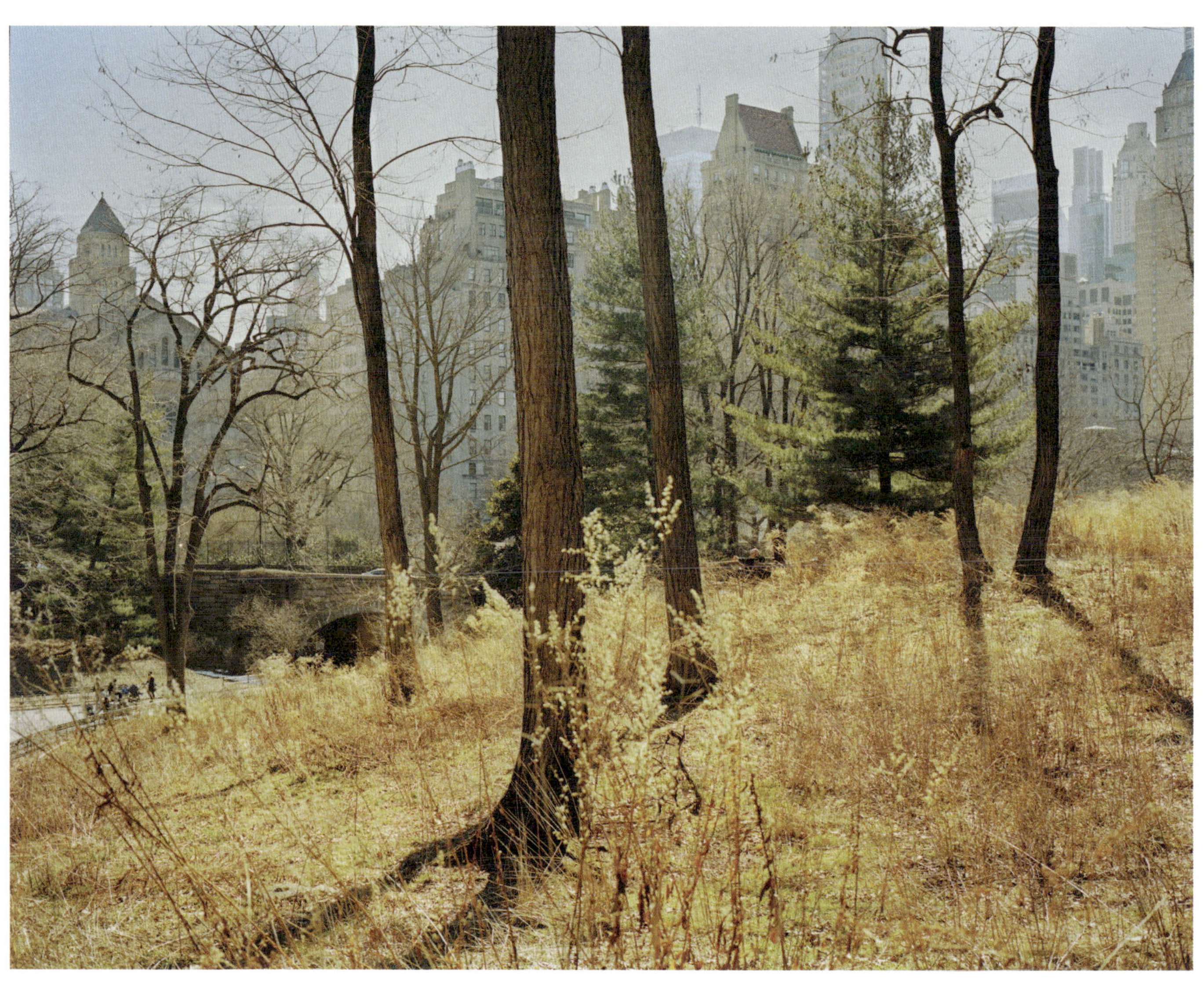

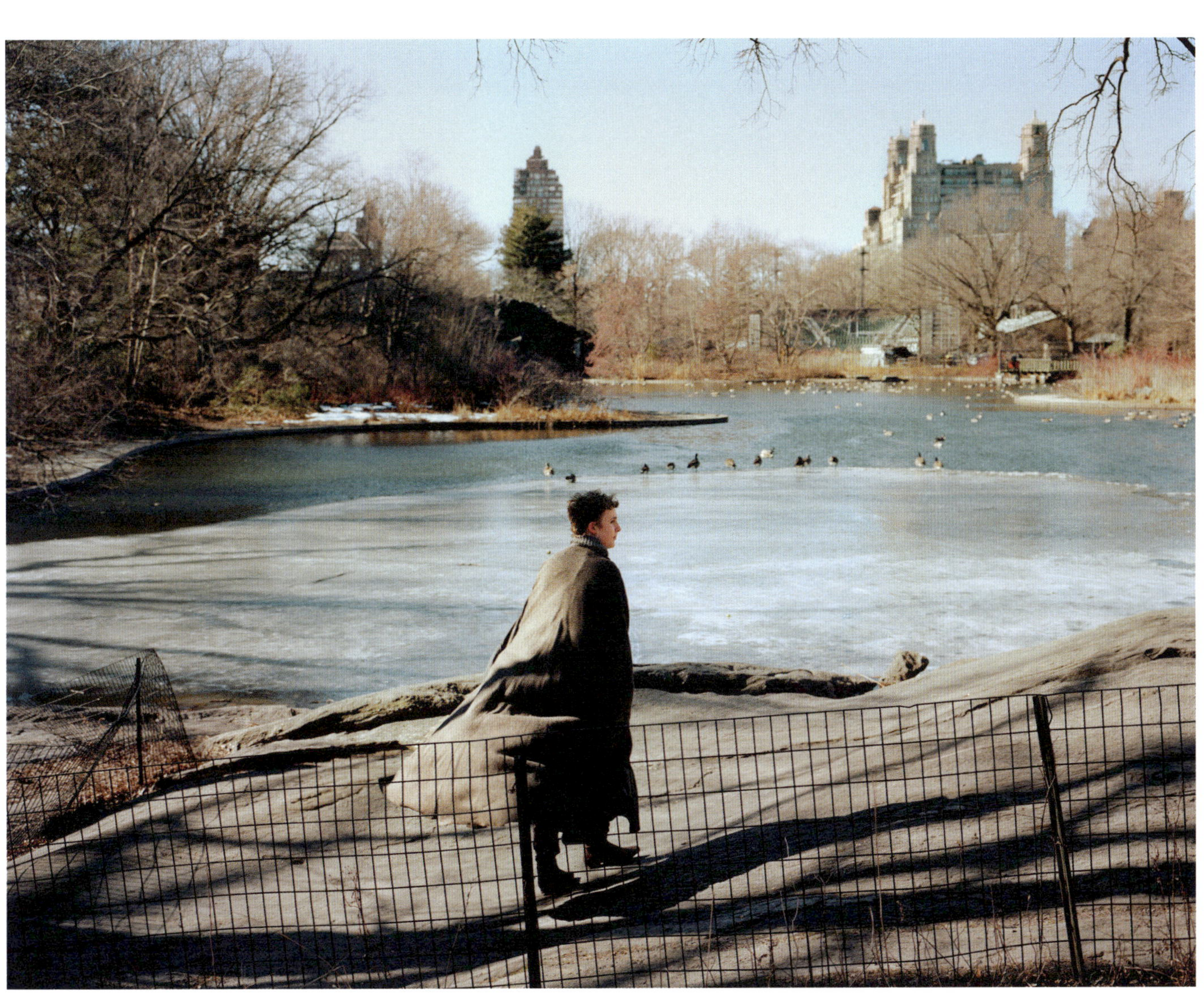

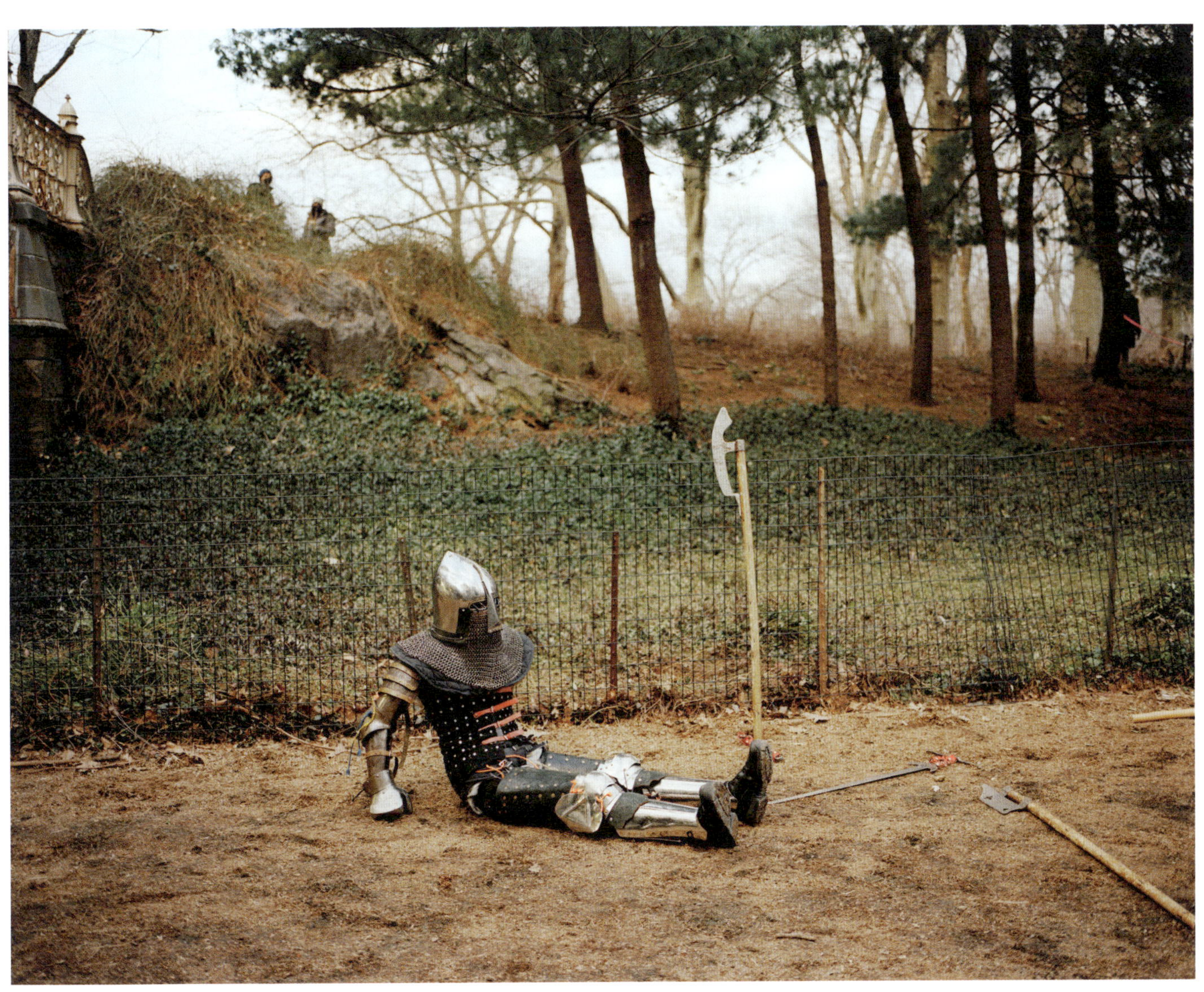

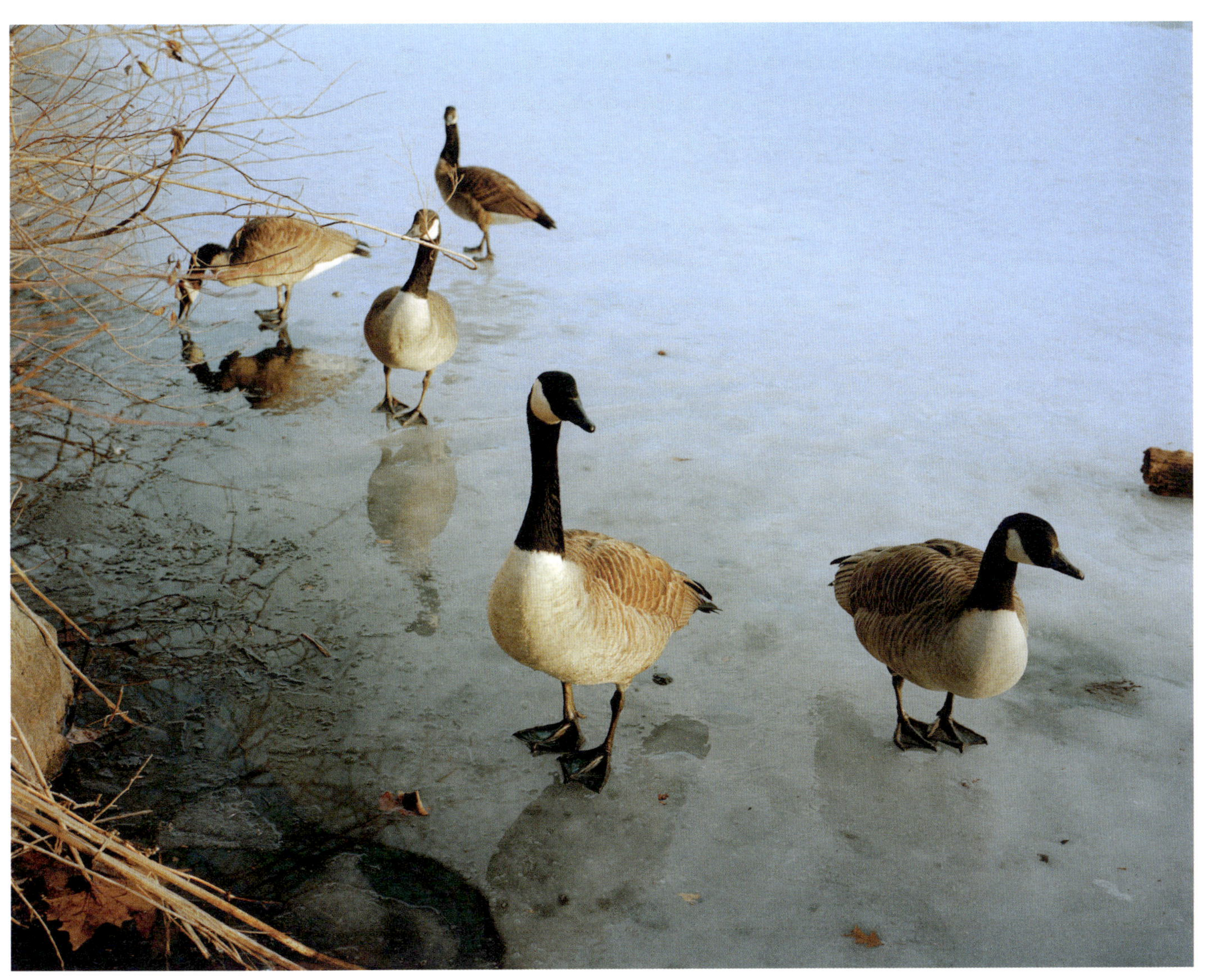

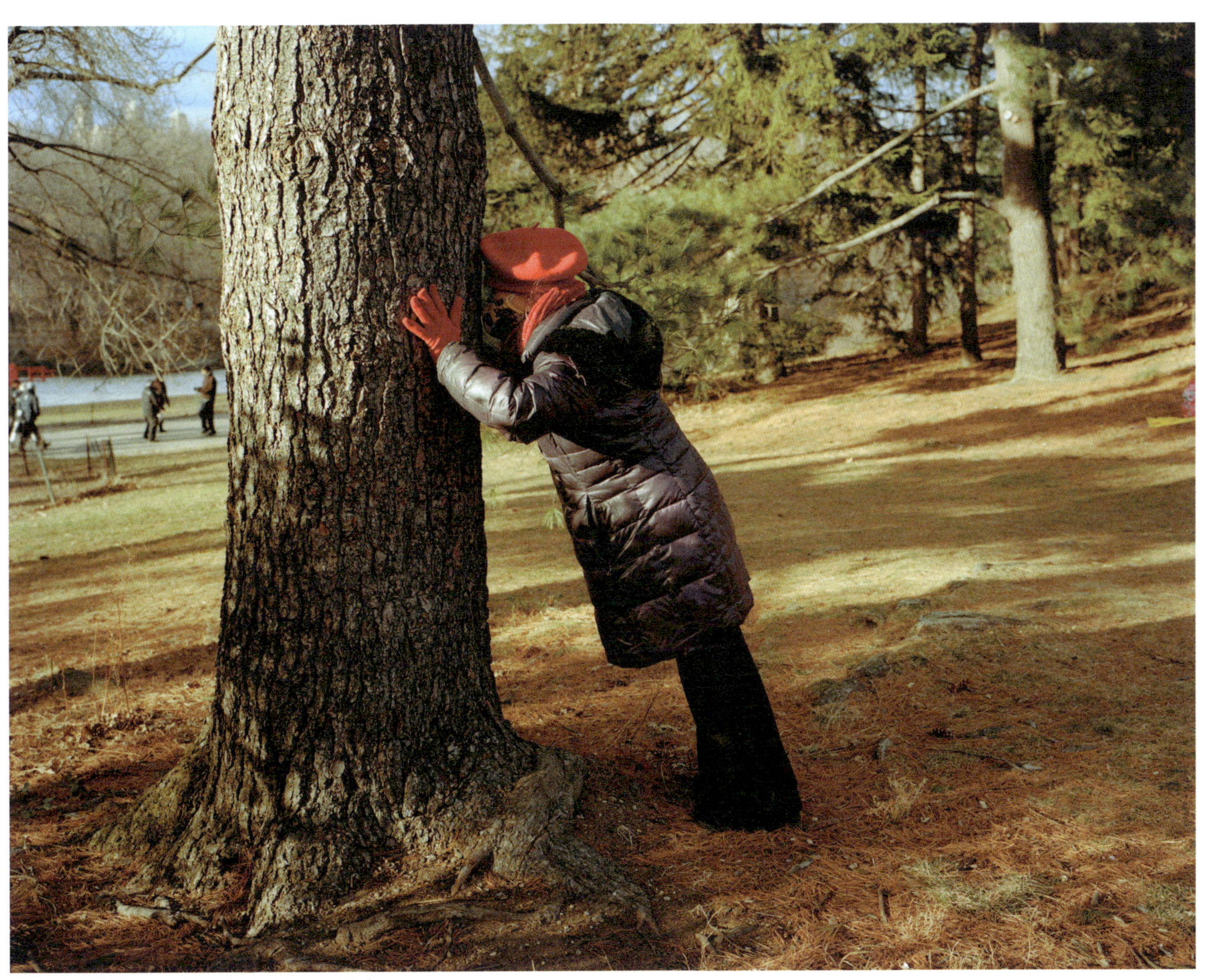

It is enough to listen
to the melodic sounds,
and admire
the sheer beauty,

and wander aimlessly
along the meandering pathways.

You aren't expected
to understand any deeper meaning,
nor the rich history
and detailed plans.

It is enough
to have walked
through the gates

and given yourself
to its embrace.

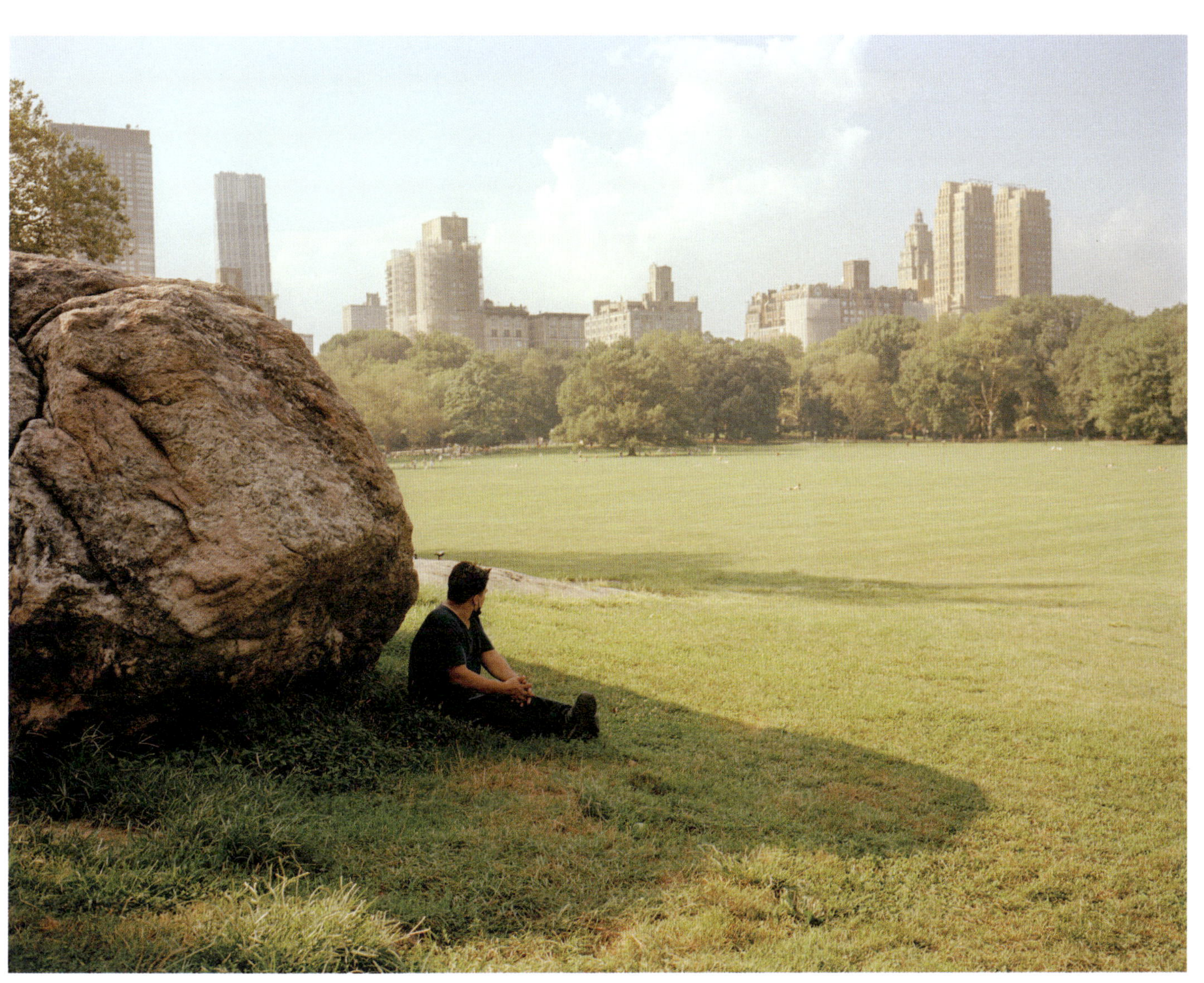

COMMON PLACE

All of these photographs were made in Central Park, New York City.

Thank you to:
Matthew Beck, Rehab Eldalil, Clarissa Fragoso Pinheiro, Dana Golan, Camille Lenain, Hayley Lohn, Sara Messinger, and Teun Van der Heijden.

Alanna, Leslie, Brenda and George Rossi.

My professors and classmates at ICP for their initial guidance.

Jesse and Thomas for believing in this work and working hard to bring it to life.

Lastly, the strangers I met in the Park who gave me so much of their valuable time.
I am eternally grateful.

•

All photographs by Scott Rossi.
Book design by Thomas Coombes, Guest Editions. Additional editing by Scott Rossi & Jesse Feinman.

First edition, first printing 2022.
Co-published by Pomegranate Press USA (POM049), and Guest Editions UK.

Printed in the United Kingdom by Colt Press.

scottrossiphoto.com
guesteditions.com
pomegranatepress.club

Any Life You Choose